The Butterfly Hours

ALSO BY PATTY DANN

FICTION

Mermaids

Sweet & Crazy

Starfish

NONFICTION

The Baby Boat: A Memoir of Adoption

*The Goldfish Went on Vacation: A Memoir of Loss
(and Learning to Tell the Truth about It)*

THE

Butterfly Hours

TRANSFORMING MEMORIES
INTO MEMOIR

PATTY DANN

SHAMBHALA
Boulder • 2016

Author's Note: The names and certain identifying features of some people portrayed in this book have been changed to protect their privacy.

Shambhala Publications, Inc.
4720 Walnut Street
Boulder, Colorado 80301
www.shambhala.com

9 8 7 6 5 4 3 2

Printed in the United States of America

♾ This edition is printed on acid-free paper that meets the American National Standards Institute z39.48 Standard.
♻ This book is printed on 30% postconsumer recycled paper. For more information please visit www.shambhala.com.

Distributed in the United States by Penguin Random House LLC and in Canada by Random House of Canada Ltd.

Some of the pieces in this book have been adapted from previously published work in the *New York Times*, the *Boston Globe*, and *Dirt: The Quirks, Habits and Passions of Keeping House* (Seal Press).

Designed by Steve Dyer

LIBRARY OF CONGRESS CATALOGING-IN-PUBLICATION DATA
Names: Dann, Patty, author.
Title: The butterfly hours: transforming memories into memoir / Patty Dann.
Description: First edition. | Boulder: Shambhala, 2016.
Identifiers: LCCN 2015044685 |
ISBN 9781611802887 (paperback: acid-free paper)
Subjects: LCSH: Autobiography–Authorship. | Biography as a literary form. | Narration (Rhetoric) | BISAC: LANGUAGE ARTS & DISCIPLINES / Composition & Creative Writing. | SELF-HELP/ Creativity.
Classification: LCC CT25 .D367 2016 | DDC 808.06/692–dc23
LC record available at http://lccn.loc.gov/2015044685

For my students,
who are my teachers

Contents

CONTENTS

Introduction

I HAVE TAUGHT memoir writing to butchers, bakers, and candlestick makers who hail from Brooklyn, Sioux Falls, and Beirut. My students have survived wars and marriages; they have crossed deserts, oceans, and centuries. But in this time of tell all and tell everybody, I still meet people who have kept secrets for fifty years. After several decades of my listening to their tales, they have given me the courage to begin to tell my own, not a wild and shocking story, but the small story of my life on earth.

When I started teaching memoir writing workshops at the YMCA, I heard stories from a woman who hid in a cellar eating tulip bulbs as the Nazis marched overhead and from a frail man who learned to read from soup cans in an internment camp in California. Now I hear stories from a woman whose mother labored in a Barbie factory in Hong Kong, from the last surviving son of a farming family in West Texas, and from a woman from Ecuador who remembers the taste of Tabasco sauce that was used on her mother's breast to push her aside for the next baby on the way.

What began as a way to help my students uncover their stories evolved into a parallel quest I started when my first husband, Willem, became sick with brain cancer. He was Dutch and knew many languages, but as he began to lose more words every day, he whispered to me, "*Lieveling,* we have to remember the butterfly hours." English wasn't his first language, and he called pinecones "pineapples," so I cannot say I understood completely, but I was entirely sure what he meant.

For years I had little interest in "true life" books, as my son used to call nonfiction. But at each step through the storms in the world, I have found myself writing more and more "true life." I took a "taste of my own cookie dough," as Willem used to say, and began to do the memory exercises from my workshops myself.

Now each day I do the same assignments I give my students, one-word memory triggers like "Table" or "Car," with time to "saunter in the woods," as Thoreau would say. These assignments are a way to stitch together the patches of my life.

I've now taught my workshop at the YMCA for more than twenty-five years. The class description reads:

Lifestories: For people who want to write about their childhood as well as their more recent past. Whether you are a published writer or last wrote in a diary long ago, you are welcome in this class. Mark Twain said, "The difference between the almost right word and the right word is the difference between lightning and a lightning bug." Finding the right word is the goal of this workshop. Suggested weekly assignments will be given to help trigger memories.

The class is as basic as writing your story and then reading it aloud—as simple as writing in invisible ink made from lemon juice, then holding it to a flame to read the words. When you write about a memory you begin to remember more fragments of your life; when you read it to others you remember even more.

I had one student who took my workshop for fifteen years. Every time I gave the assignment of "Kitchen Table," she wrote about when she was three years old and her father set down his glass of wine, left the table, and walked out of the house. She never saw him again, but she remembered the smell of burned coffee grounds in that room. She wrote that story and she read it aloud each time she did the assignment, and each time it was different. Each time she added more

3

details, and the last time she wrote that story she read a line she had never written before. She wrote, "It is only later that I learned that the man at the table when I was three years old was not my father at all, but my mother's lover. My father had died the year before."

I never learned how much later she learned this truth, but it was in the writing and the rewriting and the reading aloud, year after year after year, that she was able to get to what had happened that night, like when one sings a song over and over, until finally the pitch is right.

It is what happens when two friends walk each other home telling stories far into the night. It is as easy and as difficult as, "Hear my story. Once upon a time . . ."

∽◆∽

In this book I offer the ten lessons that have rung true with me through every season of writing. Within each of those chapters are various assignments using concrete writing prompts, often just one word, to help trigger a memory. With each assignment, I offer samples of my students' writing as well as stories from my own life: a Jewish girl growing up next door to a convent with a father who was a TV executive and a mother who didn't let us watch TV; my marriage to a Dutchman and the adoption of our son from

Lithuania; my husband's tragic death and my new marriage to a southerner; and what it's like to suddenly be a mother to three sons.

Some of my students are published writers, and for some English is their tentative second language, but they are all transformed by their own words.

The first assignment I ever gave was "Food." I left the class as they wrote for ten minutes. After the allotted time, I asked them to read their work aloud. The stories flowed from an Irish painter who wrote about having a hearing aid the size of a cigarette pack when she nursed six babies; a man who told of a parakeet that ate ice cream and spoke French; a woman who hid from Nazis in a barn for an entire winter with only chestnuts to eat. I was enchanted.

Early one morning, a student named Sulyn came to my class before anyone else arrived. Her pale face had fine lines like calligraphy. She had been born in the southwest corner of China. Her felt hat was as wrinkled as her face. She had a sandwich wrapped up in wax paper and secured with a rubber band, which smelled of pickles and fish. She offered me a bite. She broke off a piece, and I almost cried from the fierceness of it.

When class started she read aloud. "We had rice balls every day growing up. Some days that is all we ate, and they always tasted a little bit of gunpowder from the firecracker factory where my mother worked. There were five of us girls. Small Happiness—that is what my mother called us. If she had had a boy, that would have been Big Happiness, but all my sisters died. I am here in this class now. I am going to write my head off."

My aim with this book is to inspire and excite you so that, day by day, page by page, you too will write your head off.

.

Write Out of Love or Anger

I have woven a parachute out
of everything broken.

—*WILLIAM STAFFORD*

WRITING IS A LONG ROAD. You need to be fueled along the way. Write about the anchovies your uncle made you eat off the pizza or the nape of the boy's neck who sat in front of you in Spanish class or the green jealousy you felt when he put his arm around another girl.

All good writing is a blend of memory and imagination. Writing is so grueling, you have to either hate or love what you are writing about, and sometimes both at the same time. It is this passion, whether it takes the form of intense joy or sickening anguish, that often

7

sustains writers. Writing about the simplest subjects can propel a person back and through the pain. Torture victims are often asked to write about a memory of food, and they find their way home through writing about deprivation and then the joy of warm bread and jam. You don't have to be Proust or taste a madeleine to write well. Cinnamon toast or Cream of Wheat will do just fine.

Obsession is not a pleasant emotion to live with, for you or your loved ones, but for a writer it's what gets you to sit in the chair. Take notes on the thoughts that floated up while you were sleeping, while you were swimming, while you were walking the dog, and write them down before you lose them, in a notebook, in your phone, or on your hand.

People frequently throw away bad photos. We put the good photos in frames on the wall, on our desks, or in albums. We delete the bad photos from our smartphones and computers. But when you write, your hands take you to places that are not always bright and sunny, and unless you delete or burn your work, you will write to the land of thrown-away photographs, the land of sorrow and fear, and that will be the fertile ground for some of your best writing.

Kitchen Table

I was always the smallest in my class and often the only Jewish girl, with curly hair and wild eyebrows. I grew up with my brother and sister and two parents next door to a convent called Helpers of the Holy Souls. We three kids ate dinner at the kitchen table every night before my father came home and when he didn't. I don't know when my mother ate dinner. My mother typed up menus on her Smith Corona typewriter for the days ahead, carefully creating the shopping list for the week. Hamburgers, baked potatoes, canned peas. Meat loaf, mashed potatoes, frozen brussels sprouts. When she was pregnant with each of us she cooked meals ahead of time and froze them so that during the two weeks she was in the hospital, the babysitter would have food to put on the kitchen table.

My mother was not a traditional homemaker. She was not a traditional anything. My father was a television executive, and my mother let us watch only one hour of television a week. I was a disciple of *Gidget* and the *Patty Duke Show,* and I regularly sang the theme songs of both during meals, to the annoyance of my brother and sister. Sometimes I gave up one of them to watch a half hour of the *Ed Sullivan Show* on Sunday nights.

Each weekday the fathers took the train to New York City and came home drunk, while the mothers stayed in our little town and went a bit mad. The nights my father did come home, I went with my mother to pick him up. We waited in the station wagon together, and I could quickly identify my father as he limped down the platform with the rest of the fathers. My father had had polio when he was a child, which left his right leg as thin as a stick. To me his gait was beautiful. It never occurred to me that there was something wrong with him or how much suffering he'd gone through as he grew up longing to play baseball with the other boys.

Office

My father was different at his office in the city than he was at home. At home he dug in the garden, hobbling around, his boxer shorts longer than his stained khaki shorts. In the office he wore Brooks Brothers suits and went out for lunches and more with secretaries and movie stars. He was the one who told the Smothers Brothers they were fired. He was the one who told a jittery Judy Garland that the 9 P.M. spot on Sunday night, where she sung her heart out in her last comeback, was not getting high enough ratings and she had to go. I think in some way I was always fearful my father would cancel my show.

Shoes

It was while waiting in the parked car to pick up my father from the train one night that my mother gripped the steering wheel. "It is important," she said, staring straight ahead at the railroad tracks, "to be able to walk in someone else's shoes."

From that moment, and it has not stopped since, I began to try to imagine wearing other people's shoes, because my mother said to. Sometimes I imagined I was in my father's shoes, one shoe two sizes smaller than the other, and sometimes I imagined I was wearing the black laced shoes of the nuns as they walked by our house. I imagined my grandmother in her slippers, who at ninety-three remarked about her marriage to my grandfather, "We had good decades and we had bad decades." I imagined being my Dutch husband as a little boy, in his little Dutch shoes, being told to run to the bakery for bread each time his mother was about to give birth to one of his sisters on his parents' bed.

Sunday mornings my mother insisted we had what she called "Prayers," and my brother, sister, and I would sit hunched in the living room, reading psalms and reciting Emily Dickinson poems with varying amounts of concentration. My father sometimes did and sometimes did not appear for "Prayers." My brother didn't see the point, and my little sister often just wanted to sit on my lap. My mother quoted Emily Dickinson so much I thought she was a long-lost relative. We did not talk about being Jewish.

Church, Temple, or Mosque

The religion in our house was basically made up of superstitions. Detroit was the city where my father grew up in an Orthodox Jewish home. He went to temple every Saturday and on all the Jewish holidays, but when he moved to New York he stopped. Our family never went to any temple or church. We had a Christmas tree for Christmas, although we went to my grandparents' house for Passover. Growing up next door to the convent, I didn't think it was strange that a Jewish girl spent so much time talking to the nuns, and nobody ever pointed it out to me. In fact, I never heard the word "Jewish" spoken in my house, but my mother had beliefs. If we lost an eyelash, we were told to put it on the back of our hand, make a wish, and blow it off. We were not allowed to have bananas in the house and we peeled all the price labels off everything. We were forbidden to be indoors when the sun was shining. We could not wear the color purple or boil water in a tea kettle; water had to be boiled in an open pot.

When my mother drove us fast, fast over the bridge to my grandmother's house in Croton-on-Hudson, she'd shout to the three of us bouncing in the back seat, "Pick your feet up when you go over a bridge, or it's bad luck," and so we lifted our little feet in unison and prayed we would not crash.

Scarf

On the last day of class one December morning, a slight woman with gray hair approached me after our session. She had been writing powerful pieces about being a Jew but posing as a Catholic to survive World War II when she was a teenager. She handed me a small package wrapped carefully in turquoise tissue paper.

"Please open this at home," she said.

I thanked her and said good-bye. "I won't be able to come back to class in January," she said. "I commute from New Jersey, and with the weather, well, it's difficult."

I again thanked her and said it was a pleasure working with her.

When I got home that night, I unwrapped the package. There was a beautiful turquoise silk scarf with subtle fluttering designs.

The note read, "Dear Teacher, Thank you for your class. I had never told anybody what I did during the War before, not even my husband. Perhaps one day my daughter will read what I wrote. I had not wanted to write it in class, but that time, during the War, was the happiest time of my life. My daughter has been in a wheelchair since she was four, and the strain and physical challenge on our whole family has been much more difficult than anything in the War. Someday I would like to write about that. Until then, here is a scarf for you, which belonged to a friend of mine who did not make it out."

Perfume

My mother wanted us to find a noble path, if not in religion, then certainly in literature. She taught me to read from the heavy hardback *George Washington's World* the summer before I started kindergarten. That book pressed heavily on my knees as she sat on my bed, smelling of Chanel No. 5, in her pretty blouse and skirt and stockings and high heels, and helped me to sound out each word.

My mother's own father had dabbled in Christian Science and rarely went to synagogue. Though she attended Barnard and then graduate school at Columbia, my mother was not above reading her horoscope. She got into law school, but she never went.

Storm

One April day when I was nine years old and there were threats of a thunderstorm, my mother said, "We have to drive somewhere. We'll be safer in the car with the rubber tires."

She herded my brother, sister, and me into the blue Buick station wagon and drove us fast into New York City, which we simply called "the city," as if other cities did not exist. My mother, a creative and brilliant woman, had a deep and strange fear of thunderstorms, blizzards, and even cloudy skies that colored my whole life. Curiously, she had no fear for herself, only for her children, and she traveled solo around the world during her eighties, through hurricanes and avalanches. Although Joan of Arc and Harriet Tubman have always been my idols, I have remained more of a watcher and listener in the world. As much as I've fought it, I've absorbed some of my mother's fears, so neither riding my horse into battle nor sneaking through swamplands in the dead of night was a career choice I could seriously contemplate.

On this adventure into the city, my mother drove my older brother and younger sister and me to an exhibit at the Morgan Library of the Brontë children's miniature books microscopically written in brown ink. Standing on tiptoe to see those tiny books in the glass cases, I could feel a physical longing to touch them, to hold hands with those Brontës.

When we got home to our house in the outskirts of the city (I love the word "outskirts," although perhaps soon it will leave our language), I went up to the attic that smelled of the ocean. I sat there sucking on lemon drops and cut up tiny pieces of scrap paper, then carefully sewed them together with blue thread. In these books I wrote tiny masterpieces that I hoped would be in an exhibit someday. To this day, lemon drops bring me back to the attic and to the Brontës' books.

Steal from Yourself

All sorrows can be borne if you
put them into a story or tell a
story about them.

—*ISAK DINESEN*

I F YOU WRITE ABOUT your father, open the top drawer of his bureau and show us the handkerchiefs, cigar bands, and crumbs of candy bars. Go through your closets, current and remembered, and find the shoes you wore the first day of junior high; sort through that box of photos for the one of your mother in a polka-dot dress.

Up through the 1800s, the only way for American newspapers to get the news from overseas was, of course, by ship. At first reporters stood on the docks, eagerly awaiting news from Europe, Asia, and Africa, but then people wanted the news faster. The heartier young journalists found rowboats and rowed out to the great ships to get the news. And then those who hungered to get the stories even more quickly realized if they used carrier pigeons to fly out to the ships when they neared the port, the birds could fly back to the docks with the stories taped to their legs.

That is how it is with writing one's own story. Everybody goes at a different pace and uses different styles, but everybody is trying to get out to the ship. It is those stories, whether from your real life or your family's life or what you see across the street, that are the fabric of your work.

Writing fiction is like digging holes for posts in hard earth, steadying the posts, stringing the line, and then hanging up the clothes, with clothespins in your mouth, all the while watching out for rain. With memoir writing, the posts are there, and maybe the line is strung, but you still have to figure out how to hang the clothes. In both fiction and memoir you are stealing memories from real life.

Secrets kept and then secrets revealed. Whether the secrets fall one by one, as do most autumn leaves, or in one crazy torrent in the middle of the night, the way they do from gingko trees, you have to stand by the tree.

In the 1950s it was common to see whole houses

being moved on flatbed trailers around the country. People loved their homes, and though they had to move because of work or family, success or tragedy, they would bring their precious past with them. That passion and obsession with the past are what fuel your writing. Today you might not see people carrying their houses behind them, but what happened in those houses is what they write about for generations to come.

Gloves

My mother wrote a column called "Tripping Lightly" for our local newspaper, the *Patent Trader,* that had nothing to do with drugs.

I tagged along with her on stories even before I could write, pretend scribbling on the pages of my notebook. We went to the Fulton Fish Market down on the docks in New York at dawn to hear the salty stories of the fishermen in their leather aprons, my mother with her cloth coat and fur collar, her white gloved hands, as I stood by her with my notebook and pen. I went with her to colonial restorations along the Hudson River and watched 1960s women in colonial garb make bayberry soap and candles. We went to a big vehicle training school in New Jersey and sat in the cab of a crane as it was operating. I was a cub reporter, and I loved it.

It was at the big vehicle training school, as we were stepping out of the cab, a burly guy holding my mother's gloved hand as her high-heeled shoe reached for the ground, that my mother advised me, "Typing and driving are two things a woman can never learn too early." I typed easily at ten, but the real thrill came when I was twelve, sitting on a phone book, peering through the steering wheel. When I drove, timidity turned into total joy.

Sister

One day when I was six years old I came home, and my mother was frightened that my sister was dead. She wasn't. She was at her friend's house. I told my mother to sit down in the big blue chair in her bedroom.

I went downstairs and boiled water in an open pot and put a bag of Lipton tea in the teacup, blue and white china in a floral Danish pattern. I walked upstairs and handed her the tea.

She drank it with shaking hands as I began to tell her stories, stories about sledding in the backyard, stories about playing tennis on the red clay tennis court until our white sneakers and palms and faces were stained a pale rose color.

"Remember? Remember? As long as you can remember joy," I would tell her, "you will be OK."

My mother's hands stopped shaking, and she sipped her tea.

I told her my sister would be coming home soon, and then my sister did, and we didn't tell her what had happened.

Chair

The first day of class Shirley, who had been a nun for twenty-three years, confided in me that she did not want to write about herself. Instead, she said, all her stories would be about her younger sister, who was mute. I thought this was curious, but I said she should write about whatever she felt moved to write about.

One December day she wrote a haunting story in ten minutes about how when her sister was a child she was tied to her chair in her Albany home and left alone for hours at a time.

Weeks later Shirley came up to me at the end of class as the other students filed out.

"I need to tell you something," she said. She said again, "I need to tell you something now." She could see how distracted I was.

"Yes," I said. "Yes, tell me what?"

"The sister I was writing about was myself. We took vows of silence in the convent, and I felt ashamed to write about myself. I am the sister I was writing about. I was tied to the chair as a child," and she turned and walked out of the class.

Dancing

While my mother drove me to modern dance class and ballroom dancing class and quoted Wordsworth when I was a child, my father was at his office in New York City with three televisions tuned to the three major networks all day. He ate at the Four Seasons Restaurant for lunch, and came back home at night in the dark to three unruly kids. Some nights Judy

Garland called from Beverly Hills, drunk and crying on the phone.

My mother spent five years writing her master's thesis on Wordsworth in her messy office off her bedroom that she kept locked. Then there was the cold November my mother didn't have the strength to "work on Wordsworth," as she called it, and she went "away for a few weeks," as my father called it. I took care of the house and my sister "for a few weeks." When my mother came home she did not talk about Wordsworth.

Test

My mother taught me to drive when I was twelve, with me sitting on the necessary phone books, driving the blue Buick station wagon to the end of the driveway. My sister was my passenger, and we would put pretend letters in the mailbox, stamped with S&H Green Stamps we had filched from the messy kitchen drawer. My sister would roll down the window, reach out her arm with the letters addressed to made-up towns, then put up the red metal flag to notify the mailman of outgoing mail.

When it was time, my mother drove me to my driving test in Carmel, New York. Carmel was only fifteen miles away, but I would have driven halfway around the world to a town called Carmel, because caramels were my favorite candy in the world. My mother drove fast, over the speed limit the whole way, no seat belts, with me digging my fingernails into the plastic seat and the AM radio turned up loud, the Beatles screeching "All You Need Is Love" as we rounded the corners. My father had caramels hidden in the top of his dresser drawer. I went there each day when he was off at work in the city and stood on tiptoe, scrounging around for sweets and love.

Store

One day in high school I cut classes and took the train to Greenwich Village. I wore a cotton dress and matching headband and found my way to a psychic who went by the name of Susan Seer.

Susan Seer worked in a shoe store on Eighth Street that sold heavy leather sandals and bags. There were no other customers in the store, just Susan, a tall woman who wore a long lacy turquoise dress and did not wear a bra but needed one. She came out from behind the counter, and she was barefoot, so I could not imagine what it was like to walk in her shoes. She started by saying, "Don't tell me the one about shoemakers' children wearing no shoes. My father was a dentist. I could tell you were going to say that."

I started to protest but did not say a word. I needed to know how the rest of my life would shape up.

"Sit," she said, and I sat on one of the chairs against the wall, and she sat on the little shoe-seller stool.

"Give me your right hand," she said. "Well, first give me five dollars."

I handed her a five-dollar bill with my right hand, then held out my empty palm.

"When you are thirty you will die spiritually, but you will live again. You will have your heart broken and you will marry twice. You will have a difficult life, but if you live that long, your seventh decade will be full of possibility."

Just then a hippie with a red beard walked in and asked about a leather backpack. Susan jumped up as if she were going on a date, and that was it. My fortune had been told.

Party

My parents' parties would be in the afternoons, after playing tennis. The drinks would be strong, and the laughter would be raucous. There was flirting and flirting and much more. Behind the tennis court was the barn, with holes in the roof and holes in the floor, and nobody knew when it was last used, but one day, one remarkable day, there was a suitcase resting on top of the slanted roof for a few hours. All the kids gathered around to see it and point.

"Hoboes," said my mother. "Yes, hoboes, definitely," said the other parents.

The backyard was an endless lawn where we sledded in winter and even skied, where my brother built ski jumps out of logs and packed them with snow, where my mother got the fire department to flood a piece of the lawn for ice-skating.

One springtime my father drove home from the city in his new little black Anglia, a licorice drop of a car, and my mother was gardening, and he drove right down to her on the lawn, right next to her. He honked, and she shrieked, and he rolled down the window, and he kissed her. That was the only time I saw my parents kiss each other.

LESSON 3

Read Your Head Off

Language alone protects us from the
scariness of things with no names.

—*TONI MORRISON*

READ BOOKS AND MAGAZINES and the labels on the backs of cereal boxes. In *Beloved* Toni Morrison wrote that one of her characters died "soft as cream." You can't use that brilliant line, but when a sentence like that is in your mouth, there is a possibility you'll find another to offer to the gods.

People often switch genres as they get older, of what they write but also of what they read. They will say, "I don't know why I'm suddenly reading poetry" or "I've given up reading fiction altogether." People are often surprised or even uncomfortable, as if they've suddenly begun an illicit affair if they switch writing or reading certain genres. "But I always loved fiction," they say. It is as true as swimming in a lake where the water suddenly changes temperature. It can be unsettling, but the oldest students in my class, those in their nineties, just smile and say, "And it will change again. You will see."

Genre does not matter, as long as you're reading. If you're not reading, you're not writing. Reading is part of your daily devotion if you're a writer. When you read as a writer, it is different than reading for pleasure. You are studying the craft, just as an artist must go to museums to see the great masters, and a musician must listen to Mozart and Miles Davis, and everybody should read Vincent's letters to his brother, Theo.

When you read as a writer, read a sentence and try to imagine the sounds, the touch, the taste, the smells the writer is writing about. As you write, you put yourself back together.

Divorce

When I was a freshman in college my mother said, "I can't live in a stucco house anymore," and my parents got divorced. My sister was still in high school, and my brother was off at college in California, and he stayed out there. My mother, my sister, and I moved into a wooden house by a pond, not far from our old house, and that's where men and boys began to come a-calling for all three of us.

One night, before my mother went out, she stood at the kitchen window and sighed. "It is very difficult to be a mother and a lover too."

I got a job as an intern at Viking Press and took the train my father used to take to the city, but I did not sit in the bar car. I sat on the scratchy wicker seats they had then, in my little summer dress, clutching a pocketbook, trying to figure out what had happened to my exploded family.

Each day I cleaned the glass doors of the "library"—the room with shelves of Hemingway and Faulkner first editions—and typed letters for the editors, and occasionally I read manuscripts from the slush pile, which more than once had anthologies of squirrel poetry. I usually ate my tuna fish sandwich at my desk, though once had the courage to carry my lunch bag to a rock in Central Park, where I sat clutching the bread close to my mouth, as if a bear would suddenly attack.

The first Christmas, my brother, sister, and I drove to an A&P parking lot to be with my father. We got out of our station wagon and got into the backseat of his station wagon. He was now living with his new wife and his stepdaughter, but we did not go to their house. My father sat in the front and turned around to hand us our gifts over the seat. Then we returned to our car and drove back to my mother's house.

Tennis Court

When I was a teenager I would lie on the red clay tennis court behind our house and let boys touch my breasts as my mother called from her bedroom window, "Dear, are you all right?"

After my parents divorced, my mother's boyfriends would bring her home in their cars, and they would sit there with the motor running, and my sister and I would call out the window, "Mom, are you all right?"

Before that, when we were young and pretending all was right with the world, I would make large quantities of lemonade from Sunkist cans. I would stand on a chair in the kitchen, using the hand can opener, then dropping the frozen yellow cylinder into the whirring blender and adding water. I would carefully carry the pitcher down to the table above the tennis court, while my sister carried the paper cups. We would sit under the linden tree, the tree I had adopted for my fourth-grade science class and photographed each day with my Brownie camera.

Door

I have very few male students. For some men, the crush of female adventures is too much, and they do not return to class after the first session, but others jump into the fray.

Curly-haired Roberto read quickly after just ten minutes of writing.

"My father ran away from his village in the instep of the boot of Italy after he absentmindedly let one of his family's goats fall off a cliff. He arrived in New York and moved to the top floor of a tenement in Little Italy in New York, leaving his wife behind.

"A few years later the village raised enough money for her to join him in America. The young Italian woman climbed the steps with her heavy luggage, expecting to surprise her beloved husband. She did not knock on the door. She walked in and found another woman cooking dinner. My mother threw the woman out, and by the time her husband came home from work, she had finished cooking the meal. She placed the pasta on the table. They sat down to eat and never mentioned the other woman again."

Hotel

I visited my father at the Beverly Hills Hotel when my parents were separated, a few years before their divorce. It took me four months to realize they actually were *separated,* because he never seemed to be home much anyway. I was twelve years old and had one yellow bathing suit. I sat by the hotel pool with my arms crossed, covering my new breasts, as he made telephone calls on a black phone with a long cord and chewed on a cigar.

During that same trip I also visited Batman in the *Batman* studio. A real fire broke out, and Batman in tights embarrassed me as he picked me up and we ran out of there. At night we visited producers, and I sat in a room with one producer's handsome sixteen-year-old son, who had a Beatles haircut, watching "My Favorite Martian." I was horrified when a Playtex Cross Your Heart bra commercial came on.

School

I spent my first year of college at a fancy-pants school in Vermont that used to be what we called "all girls" and now had a sprinkling of boys. It was a wild time. People were shooting up heroin in the bathrooms. The president of the college had been fired for being involved in a ménage à trois with her husband and a student. The college was captainless and rudderless at the same time.

I struggled through the year, writing anguished poetry. I hung autumn leaves from the ceiling of my dorm room as decoration and religiously went to classes, where I felt invisible. In the wintertime we had to leave our dorms because the college rented our rooms to skiers, so I pulled down the leaves. We students were supposed to have "real life experiences." I moved to Ithaca, New York, and drove daily through the unyielding snow and sleet to work in the bleak town of Auburn, one hour north. The job was in a day care center connected to the maximum-security prison. All the children's fathers were in jail for violent crimes, and their girlfriends and wives had moved to be close to them and were renting cheap apartments nearby. The little children were sneezing and lonely, missing their fathers, as they huddled together in the chilly classroom. When the children learned I lived near New York City, they begged me to take them home with me so they could live on Sesame Street.

Pipe

That fall, when I was at school in Vermont, Bernard Malamud had come to my writing class, wearing a tweed sports jacket and flannel pants, puffing on a cherry pipe after each sentence he said. He told us he would write half a novel, then take a break and write three short stories before returning to his longer work.

My mother wrote me letters every week, and I wrote her back. My mother believed in writing letters. Before and during World War II, she had a pen pal, a boy in England, Charles Goodman, who remained her friend her whole life.

"There is nothing like a correspondence between a man and a woman across the ocean. You will see."

Snowstorm

The winter I worked in the prison day care center in Auburn, the snow did not cease. One day it began to snow with a relentless whiteness. At the end of the day, a fellow teacher at the day care center whose name I do not recall, an older man in his twenties with a mustache, asked if I could give him a ride home, halfway between Auburn and Ithaca, because his car did not have chains.

At this point I was driving an old Volvo that did not have chains either, so I knew this was about more than tires. I will never know why, but I accepted his request. I was not in love with the man. We rode south side by side, not speaking. I could not see where the snowy road ended and the snowy fields began. By the time we reached the old farmhouse where he rented a room, the wind was blowing at gale force. We could get out of the car, but it took both of us to open the front door in the frigid wind.

Inside, nobody else was there. Whomever he rented from must have slept over wherever they worked. By now the roads were closed.

We built a fire in the large fireplace, talking hesitantly about the children at the day care center, saying how we hoped they would be warm. He was not a mean man. I was not scared, but I knew I would lose my virginity in that farmhouse, which is what I wanted. The first night I said I would sleep on the couch by the fire, and he slept in his own bed.

The blizzard piled the snow so high that the next morning we couldn't open the door at all. We were stranded there, he and I, for three days, and all we ate was lentil stew. The second night I lost my virginity with this man, huddled together in a sleeping bag in front of the fire. I felt no joy. I felt no sorrow. We barely spoke.

And when we got back to teaching at the day care center, we both pretended it had never happened.

Bicycle

I gave the assignment of "Bicycle," one of my favorites, one bitter cold January morning. The heat was not working in the room, so my students and I all sat around the table wearing our coats and gloves as if we were huddled around a fire, although there was no heat, just the bare table, where they scrawled away.

All of them were women except for a man named Hugo, who was from Belgium. He was actually wearing a beret and indeed did look like what a writer from Belgium should look like. He was very pale, and he read aloud so quietly, holding up his paper with fingerless gloves, that we all leaned forward in our heavy coats.

"The first girl I ever kissed died a moment after she left me," he read. "We had ridden our bicycles to the closest air raid shelter, and when the all clear alarm sounded I kissed her on the back of her neck, which tasted like salt, for we all had been sweating. I let her go ahead of me out of the shelter. She turned the corner first, and then there was the gunshot.

"The second time I kissed her on the lips she was dead."

Do Not Think of Publication or Money

The truest writers are those who
see language not as a linguistic
process but as a living element.

—*DEREK WALCOTT*

S EVERAL TIMES A YEAR someone will come up to
me at a reading or e-mail me or call to ask if they
can take my class, and early on in the conversation
they will say, "Can you help me get published?"

And then I know—the way you know when your
child is lying to you or that it is going to rain—that
after I say, "Have you written anything?" they will
say, "I want to write a novel" or "I've started writing a
memoir. I'm having trouble getting started, but when
I do, how can I get published?"

I don't think someone who has never played the piano or has had only a few lessons would say, "Do you think you can get me a date at Carnegie Hall?" But there is something about writing, like no other art form, that creates expectations, perhaps because most of us are literate and use the same alphabet to write grocery lists as we do to write Nobel Prize–worthy literature. People say, "I've always wanted to write a book" or "If I had time I'd write a book," but people don't tend to say, "If I had time I'd write a symphony or dance en pointe." The fact is, yes, you can take up writing at any age. That's one of the great joys—the alphabet is free of charge for all to use. What happens with one's writing is another story.

When you sit down to write, think of someone calling you and saying, "There's something I need to tell you. Right now." Thoughts of what to wear for the TV interview and whether you should wear your hair up or loose will cloud the page.

If you're a writer, you're a farmer. It is your job to till the soil, plant the seeds, tend to the crops, and harvest the grain. And then you have the choice—either to sell the produce to market, set up a roadside stand, or feed your own family with what you have reaped. First, you have to get your hands dirty. It's relentless and difficult work, no matter what the weather; it's often tedious; and there is no predicting whether the crops will fail or thrive.

Preserving mental health is a task not to be taken lightly when you are a writer, for it is easy to tumble down the rabbit hole. It does not matter if the book was reviewed in the *New York Times* and translated into eight languages and made into a major motion picture—publishing feels like you are walking the gangplank into the sea.

Fantasizing about wealth or success or fame aids you in no way. Writing is an art form, and there are no guarantees in art. The only thing that is guaranteed is that there is a big chance you will get depressed and/or have your heart broken. Write your heart out. Write what you need to write. Perhaps it will bring you fame and fortune, and perhaps not, but neither of these will help you go to bed at night or get up in the morning.

First Job

The summer after freshman year I went home and worked in a stationery store, running an old-fashioned cash register. I had to staple *Playboy* magazines into brown paper bags when I made a sale, and I worked side by side behind the counter with a man who hemmed his pants with Scotch tape. "Should have got a goddamn wife who could sew," he'd say. "Be sure you can sew, honey, not like my goddamn wife."

In the final weeks of August, a friend persuaded me to drive out west. For no rational reason I decided not to return to the fancy-pants college. I got in her Volvo with two other friends and headed west, each of us driving as far as a tank of gas would take us, no seat belts and no speed limit. I made a wrong turn in Nebraska, but in four days we were in Eugene, Oregon, eating corn we'd stolen from a farmer's field, cooking it on a fire we'd built from dried-up corn husks and poplar branches. In the soft rain, I walked onto the pine-scented campus of the University of Oregon carrying a fistful of adolescent poems.

The next day, I climbed the stairs, poems in hand, to the writing department and knocked on the first door I saw open. Seated at his desk was a handsome man in his fifties, with olive skin and white hair. His name was Ralph Salisbury. He waved me in, and we sat looking at my sheaf of poems. "Why don't you start with my graduate poetry seminar?"

Ralph was Native American and Irish and a World War II hero and a poet. Stumbling into Ralph's office changed my life. One day, while we were walking across the campus under the pine trees, I confided in him that I wrote best when something difficult had happened. He said, "Luckily or unluckily, you will be able to write seven or eight books in your life."

Gym Class

When I was starting a new life at the University of Oregon, we had to take five gym classes to graduate. That fall I began jogging, which was such a new phenomenon that once a woman in a Plymouth station wagon slowed down as I ran along the road and asked if I needed help.

I had a real boyfriend, Randy, from Southern California. He had shoulder-length blond hair, wore purple bell-bottoms, and owned a water bed. I never could sleep on that water bed, but Randy taught me how to make love. He was kind and gentle, and his parents had run a funeral home. Randy's father died of leukemia when Randy was five years old.

One of the classes I took was cross-country skiing, and we would ski in the beautiful Cascade Mountains with our ski instructor, a handsome New Zealander, who warned us, "Never ski alone."

One January day we got to the van that was supposed to take us into the mountains, and there was a note on the dashboard saying that our teacher was missing. He had gone skiing alone the previous weekend and never returned.

I wrote poetry and majored in art history and spent my free time at the track stadium, watching Steve Prefontaine run. He held the American record in seven different distance track events and was the heart-throb of all the students, male and female, and of the teachers as well. One spring day, as he jogged by me, he said softly, "Nice calves."

The next day he was killed in a car crash at the age of twenty-four. A few weeks later I finished college but did not attend graduation. The whole campus was in mourning for Prefontaine.

I decided to move back east, not knowing where I would go after that. Randy and I had never talked about the future, not for those three years together, not like you would expect college sweethearts to do, but we didn't know anybody who even mentioned the word "marriage" in those days without shaking their heads.

Diploma

A lovely and timid student wrote, "I went to a dance, this was in the 1950s and I was shy. I wasn't much of a dancer, but I went anyway. I went up to a young man, not to ask him to dance but to offer him a pretzel, and he accepted. We danced a little, and after the dance was over he asked if he could walk me home. When we got to the coat check, the girl handed me a parcel with my coat. The young man asked what it was.

"'It's my diploma from nursing school,' I explained. 'On the invitation it said only college graduates would be admitted to the dance, so I brought it just in case.'"

Summer Job

I moved home and again worked at the Viking Press, where along with cleaning the bookcases and running errands I read more manuscripts from the slush pile, which now included recipe books for cooking with bread crumbs. In my free time I read a first edition of *Ethan Frome* by Edith Wharton five times. I was haunted by the triangle of the couple and the young girl, the sledding, the sparseness of the prose, Ethan and his horrible wife, Zeena, and his mad love for his young niece. Trying to fix a broken pickle dish is as far as their passion gets, and then they are both mangled in that passionate sleigh ride.

As I was about to start reading *Ethan Frome* for the sixth time and September approached, I decided to go to Paris. If I was going to be a writer, I had to go.

Lunch

One October afternoon, while I was living in Paris, an American friend brought me to lunch at the de Brunhoffs' house. Laurent, a magnetic elf of a man, came down to lunch with paint in his hair from his attic studio, where he was working on the illustrations for the latest Babar books. I was seated next to him at a round table heaped with food that looked like it had been painted by Renoir. Laurent's first wife, Marie-Claude, a gifted translator, elegant with her teal suede skirts and long legs, served soup and delicious quiche. Laurent had taken over the family business from his father, Jean, who wrote and drew the first Babar books. I had lunch many times around that table, and once Laurent took me up to his studio and we stood close, so our shoulders touched, and he pointed out how the trunks of the elephant were longer in the drawings his father did. Marie-Claude would take drags on her cigarette holder and pass the large bowls of delicacies she made each day for lunch. I also took yoga classes with Laurent, or *le yoga,* as he called it.

On weekends the de Brunhoffs drove in their Citroën to their country house, and all that winter I went with them. Laurent did the driving, and Marie-Claude was in the passenger seat, with the latest book she was translating for Knopf propped up on the dashboard in front of her. Laurent's mother, a tiny woman who looked just like the old woman in the Babar illustrations, would arrive on Sundays with a box of delectable patisseries.

Their serious daughter, who wore only brown clothes and took photos of authors for their book jackets and of authors' graves, took me under her wing. We would chop wood out in the frosty yard at their house, while Marie-Claude read back issues of the *New Yorker* and smoked her Gauloises cigarettes.

Birthday

I was lonely in Paris jogging in the Tuileries. I'd been going out with an older ex-pat poet who told me the only important things in life are food, sex, and art, but he had moved on to a long line of other waiting American girls. I had gotten into the MFA program in writing back in Oregon, which is where I intended to go. I left France after a year because it was going to be my grandfather's eighty-fifth birthday party and, although if a cousin committed suicide it was not mentioned, we were not supposed to miss a family birthday party.

On the flight home back to the States, a chic Frenchman in a suit started kissing me when the lights dimmed and whispered, "I won't be able to give you much time, but the time I give you will be very good."

When I landed in New York I was confused and rumpled and decided I should not go to Oregon, but give New York City a try, although I had always been scared of the place. I did not give the Frenchman any time, good or otherwise.

First Apartment

I found a studio apartment in New York for seventy-nine dollars a month and got a job as a secretary at a music company and then at the *Saturday Review* magazine. I wore high-heeled pumps and uncomfortable suits, and each morning I rose at 6 A.M. and feverishly wrote at the office.

It was at this time that I visited my best friend, a medical student who had moved to Oklahoma City with her boyfriend. One scalding day there was a handsome boy, also a medical student, in their kitchen, sitting on a chair backward, like a cowboy—the boy-man I would soon live with.

The first thing he asked me was if I knew how Flannery O'Connor had died. He said he kept a list of how famous writers had died. When I said, "Lupus," I guess that did the trick, because when I returned to New York, he began writing me long typewritten letters. Three months later he arrived from Oklahoma and moved in with me. We lived in the seventy-nine-dollar studio apartment, where every night we heard car crashes outside the window while we read poetry to each other. In his spare time, he wrote a novel and even wrote to J. D. Salinger for advice.

I spent three years writing another unpublished novel about a girl who dressed as a boy during World War I and typing for male bosses who ranged from one who said, "I just want to get on the train with you and ride forever" to a man who threw his wet tea bag in the out box on his desk and unzipped his fly when I went in his office to take dictation.

Knife

I walked north thirty blocks to Columbia University to get an MFA in writing, even though people warned me, "Carry a Swiss Army knife when you walk from 108th to 112th."

Every day the famous writers laughed at our anguished prose and flirted with the pretty girls and boys. "Girls," drawled Elizabeth Hardwick with her Southern lips smeared with lipstick, "girls, you THINK your lives are interesting, but you are wrong, very wrong," as she dropped ashes on our precious short stories. "It is your MOTHERS"—which she pronounced "MUTHAS"—"who are the interesting ones."

In researching my book I read the Bible, both Old and New Testaments, which I had never read, straight through several times. I read a thousand pages of nun and saint material and wrote that many as well. I was in an altered state.

I did manage to go to that graduation, and the librarians threw their caps in the air and whispered, "Shhhh!" when their school was announced.

That evening my boyfriend, now a doctor, said to me after a sublime pasta dinner, "I'm going to leave you now so I don't leave you later, when we have three kids. That's what my father did." He put his pesto-stained plate in the sink and walked out the door, taking with him the letter J. D. Salinger had written to him that included the words, "A real writer has to stew in his own juices."

Dining Room Table

I always felt like a child at the dining room table. The first time I felt welcome was at the de Brunhoffs', the family who drew the Babar books. The second place was at the Hansens', in the dining room of my boss at A&E Network. I worked at A&E first as a secretary, typing endlessly on an IBM Selectric for a good man who asked my advice on what documentaries to buy for the network, and I was in heaven. I'd sit in a cubicle all day, pressing the VCR buttons with my shoe—watching stories about the Amish, foot binding, and cars that moved sideways. And then I was promoted so that my job was going to film festivals and watching more documentaries all day. And at night I swam. The smell of chlorine from my swims at the YMCA pool was so strong that now my hair and skin reeked.

The food at the Hansens' was as delicious as at the de Brunhoffs', cooked by my boss's wife, a painter, who nightly prepared a feast for a table of young writers and artists. I did not know that ten years later, a table—not a dining room table—a small glass table would fly from a windy November balcony and hit my boss on his head. I did not know that he would survive but be different.

Museum

After my breakup with my doctor boyfriend, I couldn't sleep for months. I staggered through the streets at night. One morning my assignment at A&E was to go to the Cooper Hewitt Museum and look through the filing cabinets for drawings of Victorian England to be used in "wraparounds," short segments to run before and after a BBC series that would be on the air. I was to meet a photographer in the museum archives, who would take pictures of the drawings.

The photographer at the museum was a gaunt man with a shaved head. He had just had brain surgery and was weak, so he was being helped by a smiling and fine-faced man named Marc. At the end of the photography session Marc asked me to dinner the following night.

"Oh no," I demurred. "I just got out of a relationship. I'm too nervous."

"Well," he smiled. "Then we'll just have to go to lunch now," and we did, at the hamburger place called Jackson Hole around the corner. For the next month Marc taught me how to walk through the days. Soon, slowly, I began to be able to sleep again, and one morning I awoke to Marc kneeling by the B. Altman shopping bag on the floor, separating all the confused drafts of my novel.

Necklace

When I was thirteen years old, my father gave me a pearl necklace after he came home from one of his long stints "on the coast," which meant in Los Angeles. Perhaps he had been with a lover or two, perhaps he had really missed me, but there it was in a small box from Cartier, for me, a tomboy. I kept it in the box until I got a job in television, trying to follow in his footsteps at twenty-three. I wore it to work every day over my sweater, under my suit jacket. I had three work suits, suits with skirts, not pants, some kind of knit and polyester, in navy blue, green, and brown. I marched to work in running shoes in my uniform, and I marched home each night, three miles each way, from 86th Street near Riverside Park to Midtown Manhattan. One January day there was a blizzard, and as I walked I felt something slither down my blouse. I put my hand to my neck, fumbled under my scarf, and realized the necklace was gone. I stooped for an hour, searching and spinning in the snow on Fifth Avenue, but the pearl necklace was gone. I have been searching for it ever since.

Studio

When I was working at the *Saturday Review,* I was a secretary and fact checker. One day my boss told me to call E. B. White's house in Maine to check on a quote. I did as I was told. The phone rang eight times, and when I was about to hang up, his wife, Katherine, answered it. "E. B. is in the boathouse," she shouted as if the connection were as primitive as Dixie cups attached to string, at which point I could swear I heard Stuart Little's little feet running across the floorboards.

That is the life I wanted, a husband who called me by my initials and a boathouse as my studio.

In fact, at that point I had no boyfriend and no boathouse. Instead, on weekends, just after the sun came up, I walked around the reservoir in Central Park. Tourists would hold out their cameras and say, "Please, to take a picture?" and I would. I longed to have a family someone wanted to take a picture of.

Be a Slob

Writing is a process, a journey into
memory and the soul.

—*ISABEL ALLENDE*

WRITE A FIRST DRAFT quickly and wildly, as if nobody else is in the room. You can always edit later, and you will. Write as if you're four years old, sitting at the piano, banging on the keyboard and singing loudly, typos and spell check be damned, as fast as or faster than the thoughts come to you. Somewhere in those wild notes, you will find the right words.

Writing sloppily really means writing what comes to mind—fast—with nobody looking over your shoulder. Then print out your pages and take them to another room or up the stairs or outside or to someone else's house to escape the censors in your head, mothers and fathers alive and dead who are shaking their heads in your mind. It does not matter the order of things. Moving to another room or house or café to read your writing is like arriving in Paris for the first time. You will have the ability to see it anew.

You have to do the messy part because even if you write ten pages and you only like one phrase, three weeks later, during lunch or in the middle of the night, you might feel compelled to continue that phrase. If you don't have that one phrase written down, there will be nowhere to begin.

Talking underwater was a game my sister and I used to play involving a pretend tea party at the bottom of the local suburban swimming pool, but it is not an option for us adult swimmers, each in our own lane. We would both swim down to the bottom of the pool and sit there, screaming our secrets to each other. Nobody above water could hear us, and we really couldn't hear each other. Writing freely should feel like that, like screaming loudly and freely underwater. Then we would surface and swim next to each other like sea horses in a race with no finish line. Authors should do that too, without racing with one another.

Mail

Thirty years ago I moved to an apartment building in New York City where I could see a slice of the Hudson River and where I live today. When I first moved in we got mail delivered to our door twice a day. The papers slapping to the ground made a joyful sound. By the time I was newly wed to Willem, we got mail only once a day. Willem spent the first three months of our marriage back in Amsterdam, and we wrote each other postcards every day, proclaiming our love, beautiful postcards of Van Gogh paintings and couples kissing on bicycles with baskets full of tulips. My mother had been right: there was nothing like getting letters, or in this case postcards, from a man across the ocean. I would stand in the lobby as the mailman sorted the mail, and sometimes he handed me a beautifully stamped card and bowed. It took just three days to get a postcard from Amsterdam, if my husband put it in the right mailbox. Saturdays were special, because it meant I would be going the whole next day without hearing from my love, so Willem calculated and sometimes sent me two.

Notebook

Yesterday I opened a small spiral notebook I carried to Holland the first summer I was a bride. I read:

July 11, 1991—Mom, Grandma, Cilla, Dad, M. Tessa.

We played Ping-Pong outside in the cottage in the Dutch July sun, and each time we hit the ball we had to call out the name of a color from a box of colored pencils we'd gotten as a wedding gift.

> *African Violet*
> *Alice Blue*
> *Alizarin Crimson*
> *Alloy Orange*
> *Almond*
> *Amaranth*

Afterward, we sat outside holding hands on rocking chairs by the Ping-Pong table, under the sunny northern skies.

July 30, 1991 Friesland

Potatoes, meat, kohlrabi, outside dinner with Noor & Geert at 9 P.M. with the sun still blazing. We dragged the Ping-Pong table outside and played five games. Raked my wild hair with my fingers in the breeze. I won three. Willem won two. Took night train and arrived at the Amsterdam house on the canal at midnight. Came back to a sloppy mountain of mail [that] had been put through the slot in the door. Had to hang the "klamboe"—mosquito netting—over the bed to keep the mosquitoes away.

July 15, 1991

Last year when we were in the Netherlands, it was the 100th anniversary of Van Gogh's suicide and the whole country was paying respects. They even made paper money, guilders with Sunflowers *on them, and phone cards with paintings of* Starry Night.

Idea for an art exhibit—refrigerators are covered with magnets of animals and when you open the doors, the walls and shelves are covered with photos inside. I have started with a photograph of a mother and baby elephant in my refrigerator in New York.

Yesterday we went to a new restaurant in Amsterdam and had lemon custard French toast.

Emergency Room

One Sunday afternoon Willem came home with his left hand dripping blood. He had been in the Bronx playing field hockey, which he loved to do, with his team that was full of men from all over the world who grew up playing field hockey, cab drivers and professors from Trinidad, India, all over Asia and Europe. All had gone well until he got smacked in the hand with someone's stick. We spent four hours in the emergency room. It was overflowing with people who sat dazed, bruised, fevered, and demented, staring at a golf tournament on a television set hanging from the ceiling. After two hours I asked the security guard if we could please watch something else. I felt like Jack Nicholson in *One Flew over the Cuckoo's Nest,* desperate to watch the World Series, yet in fact it was *My Fair Lady* with Rex Harrison and Audrey Hepburn that calmed us down, and although none of the other patients cheered, nobody voiced any objection.

Snow

In the snowy winter of 1994, I cross-country skied across Central Park to take fertility treatments with an Iranian doctor, but later a miscarriage put a stop to that. Willem and I filled out the paperwork to adopt a baby from Lithuania. The next year, in 1995, a tiny baby girl was born and brought to the cold orphanage in Lithuania with pale yellow stucco walls. She was swaddled tight, with a piece of faded rough cotton cloth as a diaper, no safety pins.

We got the call that we would be able to travel to meet her, our baby, whom we named Naomi. We had no photographs of her, but we fell in love with the thought of her tiny feet. I bought a line of tiny puffy dresses, which hung in the closet like cupcakes, next to one faded brown and white cotton dress decorated with daisies my father had brought me from England thirty-five years before.

A month after that joyful call, we got another call from our lawyer in Connecticut. Naomi had died from pneumonia in the snowy Lithuanian night. I stood at my New York City window, watching a lone tugboat with Christmas lights chug up the Hudson. When I learned Naomi had died, I thought of the first line of a book I would write about adoption. "I'd wanted a baby since I was eight years old. Sometimes it was tiny whispers behind my ears, and sometimes it was a longing like a wound."

Hospital

A year after filing the paperwork, we went to Lithuania to adopt our son, who spent a week in April 1996 in the hospital for foundlings, struggling to breathe, while Willem and I had dinners of omelets, beet and herring salad, and borscht at an outdoor café. The women, who had been bundled to protect themselves from the harsh winter, now looked like movie stars in their impossibly tight jeans and T-shirts and high, high heels. My attire would best be described as rumpled. There we were in the twinkling evening light of northern Europe, while our new son, with cotton in his ears, was being pushed around the hospital in a kasha cart by older orphan girls.

Guidebook

Before we went to Lithuania to adopt our son, I had trouble sleeping. I would sneak into the bathroom and lie in the dry bathtub so I would not wake Willem and read guidebooks about Eastern Europe. Lithuanian is one of the oldest surviving languages in the world, and it's related to Sanskrit. There are thirty-two letters. Our baby had heard all those letters in his first months on earth, along with some Russian and Polish. I wondered if there was a word for "birth mother" in Lithuania. It's such an awkward term, like some kind of caveman talk—birth mother, birth mother—and I kept thinking of this woman, whether she was missing her son, her birth son. And did she weep?

Great-Grandparent

The day we got back from Lithuania with our nine-month-old son, my grandmother, his great-grandmother, came to visit. I was in awe watching my baby from Lithuania and his great-grandmother, whose mother had come from Poland, sitting on the couch together, eating grapes. His great-grandmother was 1,104 months old.

Stamp

One day I reached into my mailbox at the YMCA and pulled out a large envelope with a beautiful Swiss stamp of a peacock, the address written in a formal hand. It was from my student Hans, a gentleman near eighty. "Pink or blue?" he wrote. "I want to bring your baby a gift from Switzerland. Please write me at the following address," and he gave me his address at Lake Geneva. Hans had fled Germany as a refugee with his young wife.

Hans sat next to Ruth in class. They started a romance when, one day, Hans put his ankle against Ruth's during class.

Ruth smelled of ginger and wore a different silk scarf each week. When Ruth and her family had fled from Germany, her father had walked into a phone booth in Times Square, opened the phone book, and found the name Larsen. From that day on their name was Larsen, rather than a Jewish name.

When Ruth died, I learned that she was ninety years old, five years older than she had told Hans or anyone else.

Straws

When my son was a little boy, he loved to drink everything with a straw. He went through a box of striped straws every few weeks, and each time I replaced the box in the kitchen drawer. There is one box now, still in my kitchen drawer, half used, the straws lined up proudly in their striped rows. One day while he was sitting at the kitchen counter, kicking his feet, drinking chocolate milk through a straw, I asked him where he thought he would live when he grew up.

He took one more sip of milk, then said evenly, "Well, my wife will move in with me here, and you'll have to move out because we'll want some private time."

Time Away from the Computer Is as Important as Time at the Computer

Writers know that sometimes things
are there in the drawer for decades before
they finally come out and you
are capable of writing about them.

—*GÜNTER GRASS*

THERE ARE DAYS, even weeks, or certain months of the year, when you simply cannot write. Don't bother to feel defeated. Accept the fact you have time off and fill the well. Taste new foods, listen to music from childhood, hike trails you've long forgotten, try your hand at watercolors, recite the names of the presidents of the United States, and interview your elders. When you get back to the computer you will have something new to write about, or you will write about something old in a new way.

Writing on paper or on the computer is like sky-writing. It's very difficult to get perspective on it when you are close. For writers it is simply and profoundly just how to navigate through the world.

After you write a draft, putting the work in a drawer or not opening that file on the computer is one of the best ways to give yourself fresh eyes. The time away from the work can be one day a week, but it can also be a number of years.

I confess I started taking notes the moment my husband became ill, when he began to lose language in the very days my son's language seemed to burst from sentences into paragraphs. I can recall the moment I realized my husband was sick. But it was not until six years later that I was aware my life had changed at that moment. It was only then I understood that in that one moment, he became someone else, no longer the man I had married. It is this sort of moment that months, even many years, later can help in writing about your life. I believe time away, not just from the computer but from an event, can be one of the best editors.

You need to do something besides write, or you will lose your mind. Maybe your full-time job is that thing, but it also helps to do something else. I swim. When my mind is addled, I now say to myself what Willem told me, "You have to get your fin wet." My hair is always wet. In truth, in winter sometimes it's frozen, and my perfume is always a hint of chlorine.

My most treasured memories of swimming are skinny-dipping at night in a lake as a child, feeling the water change from warm to suddenly cold in the dark. Now, as an adult, I swim mostly indoors, but I carry my goggles in my overnight bag whenever I travel. As Isak Dinesen said, "The cure for anything is saltwater—tears, sweat, or the sea."

The pool is where I exercise, but it is also where I do part of my work. It is where I thought of the first line of my first novel: "Mrs. Flax was happiest when she was leaving a place, but I wanted to stay put long enough to fall down crazy and hear the word of God." It is where I wrote the first lines of my second nonfiction book: "The snowy night I met Willem in a synagogue in New York City, I knew we would marry, but I did not know it would last only ten years." It is where I make lists in my head to buy broccoli, wrap the twins' birthday presents, change the filter in the humidifier. Each day I try to write five pages and swim sixty laps.

When I am frightened or lonely, I dive into the water, and I could swear I have gills. I feel more comfortable in my aqua Speedo in the water than I do on land in my clothes.

Stairs

Fifteen years before, I'd fallen down the stairs in Holland and broken my thumb while traveling with my doctor boyfriend. We were riding around Europe on a Eurail pass for two months after he graduated from medical school. The physician we finally went to see in Paris had said, "Doucement, doucement," "Gently, gently," as he examined my hand, and that word *doucement* has been in my head every day since, all the time, *doucement, doucement*. I wake up in the morning hearing that word and go to sleep with it singing in my head.

I never thought, lying on the bottom of those narrow wooden stairs swearing to myself, that I would meet a Dutchman sitting in front of me in a synagogue, and marry him, and go back to Paris with him, *doucement, doucement*, for the last time in December on a free trip we'd won, round-trip tickets from an auction at his office. I never thought I would be back in Paris with a Dutch husband who was saying, "I am cold, I'm so cold" or that I would rub his back in our little hotel room and whisper, "Doucement, doucement."

Saltwater

There are moments in one's life when the river changes course completely, from saltwater to sweet water or sweet to salt. For me one of these moments was when I came home one evening from teaching at the Y.

My son loved these times. At three years of age, it was a treat for him to spend time alone with his father, who worked during the day. I always came back to a peaceful home, with my son asleep. The house was always startlingly neat and clean, the way my husband learned to make it growing up in a cold parsonage in the north of Holland. My husband was always sitting quietly at his desk, which was laid out carefully with a neat stack of papers, a feather we had picked up on the beach on our honeymoon, and his grandfather's pocket watch, poring over colonial manuscripts while listening to chamber music.

Until now.

This evening in April 1999, I came home to find my husband, Willem, in the living room, hunched in front of *Candid Camera* on the TV with the volume turned up. My son was running around the apartment in his rain boots and Willem's large New York City Marathon T-shirt, and the refrigerator door was wide open.

The amount of damage a three-year-old can do in four hours is remarkable. He had so much work to do, removing toy trucks from the toy box, spilling juice in the kitchen, scattering LEGOs in wild constellations across the floors in all the rooms.

When I approached Willem, he did not respond.

Stunned, I was drawn to his desk, which was a mess, covered in Post-it notes, as if Christo had decided to do a small art project. When I leaned in to read what was written on them, I could not decipher the tiny scrawls. In that moment I lost my husband, although the march through brain cancer toward widowhood took fifteen more months.

Desk

A young woman named Aleyda wrote about going as a little girl with her grandmother, who was born in El Salvador, to clean houses in Miami. One day the little girl sat at the owner's big desk, looking for a pencil to draw with. Her grandmother screamed at her, "¡No toque nunca nada en esa mesa!" (Don't ever touch anything on that desk!), and only in the moment of writing in class did Aleyda realize that her grandmother was so upset because she did not know how to write herself and did not know what the papers said.

Neighbor

When Willem was dying, our son would run out of the apartment and down the steps to the fifteenth floor to jump on the bed in 15-A or run down more steps to play with the dog in 12-D. And sometimes he visited a man who lived across the hall.

I would be standing on a chair, reaching for Willem's chemo medicine, which I kept on a high shelf so Jake wouldn't get ahold of it, and I'd hear the front door slam. My three-year-old was on the loose.

I knew the elderly woman who let him jump on her bed, and I'd met the people with the labrador retriever in 12-D, but one sleepless night, when Willem was tucked into his hospital bed and Jake was finally, finally asleep in his bed with the cloud and stars sheets, clutching his stuffed dog he'd begun feeding real peanut butter, I knew I had to meet the man across the hall. Friends said I shouldn't let my son visit a stranger.

And so it began. The next day I left Willem and followed Jake across the hall. I knocked on the door, and a voice said, "Door's open. Come on in."

I entered a small apartment that smelled of pine and cloves and danger and had walls covered with photographs of sailboats. Jake was racing one of his precious fire trucks on the floor in the living room.

The man was at his desk and swiveled around in his chair. I'd never seen him before. He had white hair and bright blue eyes.

"Would you like a glass of wine?" he said.

"No, no thank you. Jake, it's time to come home. Thank you for watching him."

Jake looked up from his work and shook his head.

Eventually I got Jake home, but each day he would return, and each day I would follow.

Not two days after Willem's death, we became some kind of patched-together little family, running back and forth between the apartments, causing clucking conversation in the building.

Death does that, throws people into each other's arms.

Laundry

The hot August night Willem died, I stayed up weeping and ironing his shirts in the room that had been his office, a room where we occasionally made love. As I sobbed, my tears fell, moistening the cloth. My four-year-old son, Jake, was finally asleep. The funeral home people had come earlier, and Jake and I had waved good-bye in the rain as the black van took his body away. Willem was born in a Mennonite parsonage in an area in the north of Holland called Friesland, where his father was a minister and his mother raised three daughters and Willem, without a refrigerator. Just like the Brontës, I thought when I met him, three sisters and a brother—although he was not wayward and did not have trouble with the bottle like Branwell did.

Ironing has always comforted me. As a young child I used to watch my mother sprinkle water from a

Coke bottle with a special rubber stopper to dampen the clothes. As a treat she would let me iron handkerchiefs. A month before Willem's death, while he was having brain surgery, I fled home from the hospital to do a load of laundry. I had been cleaning throughout his illness, and in many ways, although it did not save him, it is what allowed me to survive. I've often thought, in the years since his death, of opening a Mourners' Cleaning Service. I know I am not the only woman who cleans as she sobs in the night.

The long months when Willem was ill, cleaning was just about the only thing I could focus on, besides taking care of our son. Holland was the land of the clean people, and when he was well Willem cleaned as much as I do now. When Willem forgot the word for paper clip, I knew he was sick. When I came home from teaching one night and dirty dishes were still in the sink, I knew he was seriously ill.

Washing Machine

My student Sonia was born in Romania. In Romania she repaired musical instruments, but she came to the United States not speaking a word of English, and now she works as a babysitter.

"When I was a teenager we got a washing machine in our village, but every time someone came over my

father made us drag that machine up the steps so nobody would see or they would be jealous."

Slippers

The day after Willem died I threw away his old slippers, preferring to remember him by his marathon
running shoes. But when Jake saw the slippers dripping with egg yolk in the garbage, he yanked them out
and said, in all his four-year-old wisdom, "Don't throw
away anything of Daddy's ever."

When I took clothes of out of the dryer, Jake's child
pockets were full of dried-up ticket stubs and baseball
cards. When I remembered to check his pockets before I put them in the washing machine, I'd salvage
coins and leaves and broken crayons. His room always
resembled his pockets. When my son was young he
was a collector and an athlete, and he watched WWE
wrestling on TV.

"Mom, there are three main kinds of wrestling,
Raw, Smackdown, and ECW," my son explained
patiently.

Radio

One night I was in the kitchen, listening to NPR on
the kitchen radio as Jake was sprawled on the couch,
watching his heroes.

I washed the dishes and listened to Mozart's Flute Concerto no. 2 in D Major, a piece my husband used to love. I did not have a dishwasher. I had moved into my apartment years before, as a single woman, never knowing I would marry ten years later or that my marriage would telescope and I would be a widow there at forty-six. When Willem moved in we used to wash the dishes together, he in his Mennonite methodical style by my side. Actually I washed and he dried. We had been given three kinds of kitchen towels from Dutch relatives for our marriage—one set for dishes, one set for silverware, and one set for pots and pans. Now I was washing and drying dishes alone, trying to order my world and to soothe my messy soul. When we first met we took a walk the whole length of Manhattan and met a rabbi in Greenwich Village. The rabbi was walking down the sidewalk handing out leaflets, which we did not take, but when he saw us walking hand in hand he said, "You will have a sweet and crazy life together," which we did. We played Ping-Pong outside in the long Dutch summer evenings in the north of Holland, and we ate raspberries, and I rode on the back of his bicycle, laughing, through crazy traffic in Amsterdam, hanging on for dear life.

At nine fifteen that night I did what Willem would have wanted me to do. I decided to make a bold move. I put down my sponge and left my station in the kitchen of eternal cleaning. I joined Jake on the couch and watched Friday night wrestling with him. I had my first dose of frightening men crashing chairs on one another's greased bodies, fighting and fighting, good over evil, not dying of cancer, fighting until they were exhausted.

I reached out for Jake's hand, and he let me hold it for a moment before he pulled away. "Just because I see this stuff doesn't mean I'm going to do it," he said quietly, staring at the screen. "Somebody always wins. And just because you love classical music doesn't mean you do that either."

And then one night at ten o'clock, when WWE wrestling was over, my son made an unexpected move. He got up from the couch. He went into the kitchen, grabbed the mop, filled a bucket of water, and began to mop the floor, mopping with frenzy, a fierce mopping to save his soul.

We are all wrestling. We are all cleaning. We are doing the best we can.

Music Lesson

Sandra signed up for my class one summer session but never appeared. She e-mailed me and said she had been ill, but she might take the session in the fall, but she didn't know what to write about. I suggested she write about music or a music lesson. She appeared in

September, a beautiful woman with a scarf covering her head, her dark smooth skin the color of eggplant. I was not sure of her age. When I asked if anyone had brought anything in to read, she said that yes, she had written about a music lesson, and she began to read.

"I grew up in Barbados. We lived above a French restaurant. They played opera on their record player all night long. That's what I grew up listening to, not the local music, not the radio, but that opera on the record player. They liked me at the restaurant. The cook would give me a loaf of fresh bread every morning. The record player was in the kitchen and sometimes I'd watch the chef dance with one of the waitresses. When I came to New York all I wanted to do was go to the opera. I did. I was an usher at the Metropolitan Opera for thirty-two years before I got sick."

LESSON 7

Genius Is in the Breath of a Sparrow

Writing for me is cutting out the
fat and getting to the meaning.

—*JAMES McBRIDE*

SHUT YOUR EYES AND LISTEN to the church bell,
the train whistle, and the snow falling on the
roof. Open your eyes and see how children speak into
one another's mouths rather than their ears. Recall
the lilac smell of your grandmother as she bent to kiss
your cheek. Touch the dried snakeskin on the ground
and imagine the way your throat burned the first time
you tried hot peppers.

Whether your stitching is as elaborate as the
Bayeux tapestry or as simple as an Amish patchwork
quilt, the threads of your life are what you will weave

into the fabric of your story. Write down those memories of a long car ride playing cow poker, running on the beach and the sand turning to sugar, believing that the curtain dividing your nursery school classroom was the Iron Curtain, the sound of your father's belt when you were punished, the excitement of playing musical chairs when you were five years old and the fear of not getting to a chair in time. Details reveal character. Your first job is to be a watcher and listener in the world. Your second job is to find which details best reveal the people in your stories. Some details, although real, might not honestly show a character. If you don't use enough details or you use too many, you cannot see or hear the person or place you're writing about. Choosing which details to use is one of the most challenging jobs of a writer.

Once my ninety-two-year-old aunt told me that she hated the heat. When she was a child in Detroit, growing up as an orthodox Jew and wearing heavy, dark clothes all year around, she would sit on wooden chairs with her mother in the basement before the air conditioner, rocking back and forth on the cool dirt floor. As she talked about the stories of her life, I found myself nodding. I too am uncomfortable in the heat. I too long to rest my feet on the cool dark floors. This memory sent me to my computer, where I wrote a short story about a little girl and her mother learning the secrets of a forbidden love at the same time.

Memory is obviously tricky business. In my case I have always lied a little. When I was three I used to tell my mother stories to calm her down, or at least that was my plan. Lying a little comes easily to some people, but not to others, and serious journalists, including my husband, express shock and awe at the thought.

"But that's not exactly how it happened," I hear time and time again, or "But when I met my brother I hadn't seen in thirty-eight years, I didn't feel anything."

I wrote about adopting our son from Lithuania. I'd written one hundred pages many times, and finally I wrote the scene in Vilnius of being handed my seven-month-old son in a cold, bare orphanage room—or Children's House, as they called it—with a lone Miss Piggy doll on the shelf.

It felt completely natural to hold my son.

"I'm very sorry," my editor wrote, "you can't lead us to this place for one hundred pages and then say, 'It felt completely natural.'"

"But it did," I protested. And then I got to work. Sometimes even memoir needs another beat, two more sentences, that's just the way it is. I ended up writing, "It did not feel like fireworks. It felt like a bell ringing a perfect chime. 'Here you are little boy, I've been looking for you for a long time.'"

That line was in fact more honest than "It felt so natural." Sometimes one lies a little to get to the truth. When I write fiction people say, "That must have happened," and when I write memoir there are always a few who say, "I don't believe it." And that's the truth.

Writing seemed to me the opposite of the way Tennessee Williams's play *Glass Menagerie* ends, when Tom tells his sister, "Blow out your candles, Laura." Writing to me is lighting them again and illuminating one's life, no matter what horrors or joys one finds.

Road

In senior year in high school I learned to drive a stick shift in a Volkswagen Beetle with Jimmy Weaver. He was lanky and blond. I was small and olive skinned. We jerked along the dusty roads of a nature preserve, with raccoons waddling across our path and walnuts falling on the roof of the car. The fourth time we stalled, Jimmy reached inside my blouse. It was at that moment that I learned how to shift out of third, and I did not stall again that day.

At twenty-eight I drove from New York City to Montreal to visit friends after my doctor boyfriend left me. After one day in Montreal, I turned around and drove south, driving with a broken heart, stopping to swim in swimming pools. I changed into my bathing suit in the backseat of the car and swam a couple of lengths in the town's public pool, to soothe my soul. Then I drove in my damp bathing suit until I could find another pool, and somewhere in New Hampshire I learned my heart would heal.

It did, and years later I married the Dutchman who bicycled as a child and learned to drive as an adult. With him I learned to share the wheel. When he died I chauffeured our four-year-old son, who kicked the back of my seat shouting, "I want my tall Daddy. I want my tall Daddy now."

Playground

Just before Christmas vacation, my son came home from kindergarten and announced he had started the Dead Dads Club. It consisted of his friend Hasani, whose dad was a transit policeman who had been killed in the Twin Towers; Keith, whose father had died of pancreatic cancer; another little girl whose father had died in a house fire; and Jake.

"We're going to write a book," said Jake.

In fact, they never got farther than the title, but the kids were drawn to one another. They told their stories in their own ways on the playground under the jungle gym or in their rooms when they came over to play. These stories of loss are what kept the children going. They were constantly in motion. As the mothers stood by the jungle gym and confided in one another, the children told their stories, not necessarily in words, but as they dashed around the playground, screamed from the top of the slide, wept while they crashed into one another. No matter what your age, the telling of the story and the sharing of the word, the sorrow, and the deed binds people. Those kids might not write about the Dead Dads Club for decades to come. And by then it's possible there will be new inventions to write on or with, and ink and paper will be distant memories. As they get older that distance, that time away, will bring new perspectives and new tellings of those screamings in the playground.

Sometimes on those cold playground afternoons with the dark falling way too soon, I would remember when I was newly married and Willem was healthy and I would meet him at the subway wearing only my raincoat.

Dream

When my son was young, after his father died, he always had trouble sleeping. The day before his first day of kindergarten, a few days before September 11, 2001, he held my hand as I sat exhausted on his bed, reading to him sweet children's book after sweet children's book.

"Mom," he said. "Mom, a plane can't crash into a building, can it?" and I rubbed his back and said, "Of course not. Now get to sleep."

A few years later, when he went on sleepovers at friends' houses, before we had cell phones, he would make his way to the kitchen of wherever he was and call me at 2 or 3 A.M. "Mom," he'd whisper into the phone, "Mom, tell me something to dream about," and I would tell him a story about when we met him in the orphanage in Lithuania and the nurses would chant, "NBA! NBA!" because he had such strong legs, or when his father used to ride bikes in Holland along the icy canals and pretend he had eight brothers and they all rode together in the Tour de France, and slowly, slowly, he'd calm down.

Gun

Lauren began taking my class at eighty-five. The first day Lauren read, she read aloud quietly, with her head bent, of her father killing himself with a shotgun in the next room and from then on her mother coming to sleep in her bed.

The class was very still for a moment after she read before we began to talk about the writing. I always insist it's not a therapy group, that we're there to talk about the writing, not the subject matter, but sometimes, as it was that day, it is excruciatingly difficult.

After class Lauren came up to me and said she thought she would be able to sleep easily for the first time in her whole life.

After Lauren left the room I bent my head to my iPhone and read my e-mail. There was one from a name I did not recognize, but I opened it anyway.

"If this is the person my brother went out with in college, I am sad to tell you that Randy has died of leukemia."

I sat alone in the classroom, reading the e-mail over and over, remembering those innocent days lying on his water bed, remembering when he told me about his father, who had died of leukemia when he was a little boy.

Widow

Although the day I adopted our son in Lithuania was the happiest day of my life, I did turn to my husband as we carried our baby from the orphanage and say, "You'll take him to soccer, right?"

"Of course, *lieveling*," he said.

My son was named after a Dutch soccer player, and following the strange magic of namesakes, he's obsessed with the game.

He did not arrive in steerage, hungry and cold; our son was welcomed by a uniformed immigration officer at 3 A.M. at Kennedy International Airport on a humid Father's Day in 1996. The officer said, "Welcome to America, baby," and swung him in her arms.

Some games are an easy bike ride away in Central Park or Riverside. But we must all face our Wards Island. Nobody who plays West Side soccer escapes Wards Island. In the shadow of the Hell Gate Bridge, the island sits between Harlem and the East River. The lunatic asylum was built there in 1871. From 1850 to 1900, eight million immigrants staggered onto the island's shores, where there was a detention center for destitute and sick migrants. For years it served as a potter's field. And now, in our enlightened times, if you dare to make the journey, we have the state psychiatric hospital, the alcohol treatment center, and the sludge treatment plant.

Wards Island is the widows' albatross.

My husband never got to see his son play soccer on Wards Island or anywhere else. My initiation was on a pouring-cats-and-dogs Saturday. The island emerged in the fog like a specter from the River Styx.

But the skies cleared, and as everybody will tell you if you make the journey, "The fields are good." And as is the way on all islands, people who might not normally give one another the time of day here confess their inner longings.

"I had wanted another baby, before the divorce," one sighed.

"We're separated, but my husband's living on the same floor," shrugged another.

We stood facing our children, not looking one another in the eye, as our voices floated up in the air to join the voices of our ancestors, who arrived in America 150 years ago. As Penelope Fitzgerald wrote, "Terminal illness is a great simplifier of daily life."

Game

My student Ruth wrote about playing field hockey on an island off the coast of Germany when the Nazis took away her hockey stick. "Every morning at 6 A.M. we woke up to Beethoven being played on the Victrola. We would hurry into our bathing clothes, even in wintertime, the boys and girls, and we would race into the North Sea. We were all Christian children and Jewish children together, getting a good education and hours of sports on the beach. And then one day the Nazis arrived and took away my hockey stick and I was sent away.

"My family fled to Holland. My brother, whom we called the Professor because as a baby he wore tiny eyeglasses held on his head with a pink ribbon, he did not survive. He had gone ahead of us, across the border at night, but we never heard from him again. My brother, the Professor."

Birth Certificate

When I look at my son's adoption papers, all those papers, I can barely remember that time. International adoption is like taking baby refugees who did not ask to come to this country and putting them into tiny American Gap clothes and our families. And when they're unhinged adolescents we're so surprised, yet it happens all the time. My son had his turn, running wild, or *Rumspringa,* as the Amish would say, in graffiti-covered tunnels under the streets of New York.

Tattoos

When a student named Shy handed me a piece of writing, I was surprised to see tattooed snakes slithering up her arm. At the time my son was five years old, with soft skin and innocent eyes. Shy wrote about how she got tattoos only when something tragic happened in her life, and how she used her body as a canvas. I could not imagine having children, grown or otherwise, inking themselves instead of paper. It felt like looking at a cruel kind of graffiti. At first my own son's tattoos scared me, and for several years I could not understand him. My son's first tattoo was of his late father's birth date and death date, and the second tattoo was of his own birth date, the date when he was born from a woman he has never met, whose language he does not speak, and now I understand. Now, I feel like I am reading my son. After some difficult years, when my son got the word "Blessed" inked on his body, I felt I could begin to breathe again.

Read Your Work Aloud

Everything becomes a
little different as soon as
it is spoken out loud.

—*HERMANN HESSE*

R EADING ALOUD IS the simplest, cheapest, and most startling way to edit your own work. When I say, "Read aloud," I mean *really* read aloud, not just a quick mumble.

After you have a rough draft, read it to the trees or a kind friend, and you'll see what to cut. Family members may not be the people to show your writing to, because the words might hurt them and that will hurt you. Writing is like building a house. You need to put up an outside scaffolding to get to certain places, but then you have to carefully take that structure down.

When someone calls you on the phone and tells you a story or sits across a table from you and confides his or her woes, you don't have a script. You listen, intently if it's interesting. But if your mind wanders, that's what you need to edit in a story.

Another great way to edit is to have someone else read your work aloud to you, someone who has never read it before, who doesn't know your intent. This way, when they stumble over a word, you will hear it clearly and not self-correct it the way you might if you were reading it aloud yourself.

In twenty-five years of teaching, I have never had a student say they didn't have anything to write. After each person reads aloud I say, "Thank you" and do not comment, no matter how dramatic the reading was. Each reading is an offering, sometimes never spoken aloud before, and sometimes never thought of before. Often people come to class determined to write about one portion of their life and end up writing about something else entirely. It takes every student a different amount of time to get to the marrow of his or her life. It's like walking on a beach with a metal detector. Sometimes you strike gold the first time out, and sometimes it takes years.

Learning idioms in other languages is a great

way to exercise your writing skills. "Tomber dans les pommes"—literally, "to fall in the apples," but meaning "to faint"—is a phrase I say over and over in my head because I like that rhythm. Getting those rhythms going in your head and saying them out loud are wonderful ways to start your writing day.

My oldest students have begun to remember poems and songs from their childhoods, and often they are in languages they first heard other than English. My mother made us memorize Emily Dickinson poetry, and those poems are not just in my mind, they are in my hands. Good writing does that. It moves straight to your hands, and then when you write yourself, perhaps a trace or a word comes through to your pages.

Nightgown

A few years after he died, I felt the need to write about Willem dying. Michael, who is a journalist in Baltimore, felt compelled in the wake of his wife's death to read books on grief, which hadn't been my response. It was all I could do in those days to make a cow costume for my son's school play. But my publisher forwarded me a link to an essay Michael had published about grieving, which included a review of my book that had been published days after his wife died.

I read it online at 2 A.M., sitting alone in my nightgown, barefoot and shivering, on a winter night last year. Reading it, I felt a complete love for his late wife, Nancy, who was an art historian, just as Willem had been.

In the essay, which included reviews of works by better-known widowed writers, Michael quoted a passage of mine about a widower I had met as a teenager who still had his dead wife's clothes in his closet. I had been spooked at the time, never imagining that at age forty-six I would have a closetful of my dead husband's clothes and that it would seem right.

I wrote to him: "Dear Mr. Hill, It's an honor to be included with such wonderful writers. I am sorry for your loss."

He wrote back, commenting on the passage in my book where I describe how I kept buying basil at the grocery store the summer Willem was dying and how the smell of basil got me through those months. Since his wife died, he wrote, he didn't think he could plant a garden again.

Soon we were exchanging e-mail messages with "re: grief" in the subject line. We corresponded for two months, starting with those first cold weeks when Michael would return to his empty home, his children off at college and now Nancy gone, and struggle to shovel the icy driveway. Eventually the subject lines changed to "re: thumb-stack of pancakes" and "re: bolts of cloth."

One night my son appeared at my desk at midnight, when I thought he was asleep, while I was restlessly writing e-mail messages.

"I see how you get, all flirty-flirty with Michael," he announced.

Library

Michael was coming to New York in a few weeks, to see Joan Didion's play adaptation of her memoir *The Year of Magical Thinking*. Did I want to get together for coffee? I agreed to meet him at the Morgan Library, where I had seen the Brontës' tiny books all those years ago.

Two days later I panicked. "I have a middle school meeting all day," I boldly lied. "Perhaps another time."

But then a friend advised: "Go. You've been scared your whole life. Go."

Another said: "A man married that long, twenty-seven years, will never get over his wife. Aren't you jealous?"

"No, it's the opposite of that," I said. "I love her. She would have been my friend. I don't want him to let her go. The four of us would have been friends."

I wrote Michael and told him I could get away for an hour. "How will I recognize you?" I asked.

"I'm five foot nine and need a haircut," he replied. "I'll be wearing a baseball hat. And you?"

I wrote, "Years ago, when I was in Oklahoma, I met a man who said: 'You look like Bonnie, you know, Bonnie and Clyde. She was a little woman like you, with messy hair.'" I added, "Not Faye Dunaway."

Baseball Hat

I waited nervously for Michael at the door of the Morgan Library until a man of his description walked in. I leaned forward and put out my hand. "Michael?" I said.

"Yes," he said, shaking my hand. We talked for several minutes, and then he said, "I'm sorry, but how do

I know you?" And we realized he was not the Michael I thought he was. I was relieved and disappointed. He was a nice man, but I felt no magic.

Five minutes later another man in a baseball hat walked through the door. This was the man I had been writing to day and night for two months, who liked the words "bolts of cloth" as much as I did.

We did not look at any exhibits at the Morgan Library. I cannot even tell you what the exhibits were. Instead we sat side by side at computers, clicking randomly on virtual tours, and showing each other pictures of our sons.

"Don't you have to get back to the middle school meeting?" Michael asked over lunch, while I pushed my food around.

"No, somebody can tell me about it," I demurred, staring at his wrists.

Photograph

For our second date, we decided to go on a Circle Line cruise around Manhattan. As we filed onto the boat, a photographer took our picture. We sat on deck in the sunlight, with German and Japanese tourists seated next to us. The breeze was soft; the guide made garbled announcements about Henry Hudson and the Little Red Lighthouse, and Michael touched the back of my neck. When we got off the boat all the photos of the passengers were hanging up for sale. There we were, a middle-aged widow and widower, in love.

Button

It was almost time for Michael to plant his spring garden. A button had broken on the cuff of his shirt, and as he stood with the cracked button in the palm of his hand like an offering, I could see him missing Nancy.

I hesitated, then went into the back of my closet and pulled out one of Willem's shirts. Although I'm no Betsy Ross, I retrieved my box of sewing things, full of threads and needles from Willem's mother's Dutch sewing kit.

Working carefully with the tiny scissors, I snipped a button off Willem's shirt and sewed it onto Michael's cuff.

Ribbon

Willem died sixteen years ago. He was fifty, Dutch, a marathon runner, as graceful as a heron. Then one day, while a spring breeze rustled the curtains, he gazed at me and said meekly, "Who are you?"

I am now older than he was when he died, as is my second husband, Michael. A wedding photograph of Michael and his late wife, a beautiful reddish blonde, sits on my bureau. Some people find it strange that I would have such a photo on my bureau. I do not. These people are our stories, our past, and the parents of our children.

"I would like you to meet my parents," Michael said several months after we met. I had seen pictures of them. His father, at ninety, is a federal judge, still active on the bench. His mother, who had been a ballet dancer but now had Alzheimer's, was still married to him.

They fell in love and left their small towns in South Carolina to go to the big city of Atlanta. They were a mythical couple whose friends soaped "Just Married" all over their 1940 Plymouth. They washed it off, or so they thought. But the "Just Married" message on the roof remained, faded but defiant, baked into the paint and reappearing whenever it rained.

I brought her pink ribbons for toe shoes as a gift, to see if she remembered, perhaps the color, a sensual memory from long ago, twirling and smiling in the sunlight. She thanked me, taking them lightly in her fingers. I reintroduced myself to her each time I entered the room. Before I returned to New York, Michael's father hugged me and said in his South Carolina drawl, "Welcome to the family."

I told his mother I loved her son.

"We enjoyed having you here. We'll miss you," said his mother, holding the ribbons, although it was not clear to me if she remembered sewing similar ones to toe shoes long ago.

Soup

Michael's early e-mails to me were so long I teased him he was weaned on alphabet soup. To me his language felt like a big house with porches on every floor, while I struggled to add more words to my spare New York flat, but we've written a screenplay together. When we stand in the garden he tells me about eating scuppernongs (grapes) in South Carolina and I talk of growing up next door to the convent in the North. We also talk of Willem, who ate raspberries under the Dutch sun at 11 P.M. in July, and Nancy, an Italian American, and her blue-crab picnic cookouts at the Maryland shore.

Honeymoon

On my first honeymoon, to the Dutch Antilles island of St. Eustatius, my husband, Willem, brought a pair of scissors with which to clip newspaper articles. My second honeymoon was a road trip through the South. Though I did not bring scissors, I needed to document the whole trip, driving north, night and day, day and night, with the hot summer breezes at our necks. I have the menu from Jestine's Kitchen in Charleston, where we shared a pecan-whiting sandwich, black-eyed peas, and fried okra. I have postcards of a painting titled *A Good Man Is Hard to Find* from Flannery O'Connor's childhood home in Savannah. These things are in a box, just as I have another box of treasures from my first honeymoon. I had thought I would put the box from my first honeymoon away, but both boxes rest side by side in full view on a bedroom shelf.

When I became a widow at forty-six, I began to sleep diagonally in my bed. When I married Michael and people asked me, "What's it like to be an old married lady all over again?" I was startled to realize I'd never stopped feeling married, even when I was a widow.

Today, at breakfast in New York, I watched Michael reading a newspaper as he sat drinking coffee where Willem used to sit. When he looked up, I hesitated, then whispered, "Do you think it's all right I have two husbands?"

"It is all right," he said, smiling. "I have two wives."

The nights we are apart, I do sleep diagonally still, but we fall asleep talking on the phone, telling each other the stories of our lives.

The South

Sharon, a Broadway actress, wrote of growing up on the top floor of a public library in New York, where her father was the custodian. She would sneak down into the stacks to read at night. When her public school class went on a field trip to the library, she wrote, she didn't tell the other children they were taking a tour of where she lived.

Summers, when she was a child, her tall, elegant father would drive south with her to Florida, to his childhood home, for vacation. They drove for hours and hours without stopping. Sharon sat swinging her legs in the backseat as her father kept his hands tightly on the steering wheel. It was only later that she realized he never stopped because he was scared, a black man with his young daughter, driving past the gas stations in the South with some bathrooms that had COLORED signs and others that had no signs at all.

Recipes

I have no desire to spatchcock a chicken. I have been known to eat large quantities of toast, and one winter I ate so many tuna fish sandwiches, I had an alarmingly high mercury reading.

Our friends warned us that when a widow and widower marry, there is always baggage, but in fact our biggest challenge has been measuring spoons.

We've been united in trying to help our three sons blown sideways by the death of a parent and have been untrained guides in helping our own elders down the mountain, but it has been in the kitchen we have finally faced our friends' warnings.

Michael and his first wife, Nancy, loved cooking, and when I hear about their meals, it sounds like Marcella

Hazan and Pierre Franey were family members. Nancy made tomato sauce and samosas and pesto; Michael prepared his grandmother's fried chicken, chili, and okra; and sometimes they cooked together. I put food on the table in my first marriage. My son did not go to bed hungry, although when he was asked to write down his favorite recipe from home for his second grade cookbook, he wrote, "Eggo Waffles."

In my first marriage I made simple pasta with sauce from a jar and salad and bottled salad dressing. Willem cooked a few Dutch dishes involving large amounts of beets and leeks. Once I rustled up a startling fire-truck cake for my son's fourth birthday, but the truth is it consisted of Sara Lee pound cakes cut skillfully, coated with a dangerous amount of red dye, and decorated with licorice strings for fire hoses and peppermint candies for wheels. In Michael's first marriage, food was the centerpiece of the home. They shared many things, but there was one domain that was Nancy's alone: baking.

I learned this the first time Michael invited me over and courted me with cooking. He made salmon, potatoes, and asparagus in the part of the kitchen that was his domain, the outdoor grill. Along with cooking on the stove, he will cook out in every season, frequently standing under an umbrella or with boots on in the snow, and often using a flashlight.

The meal was delicious, although at that point he could have served an old shoe and I would have swooned. As we ate our last savory bites, Michael said, "There's ice cream for dessert. I don't bake. Nancy did the baking."

Fine with me. I was in love with the man, and who doesn't like ice cream?

Cake

For seven years, Nancy's baking tins and bowls and beaters and sifters and measuring spoons were poised for action in the drawers, albeit a bit dusty, like unused toys soldiers ready to fight.

Michael's sixty-fourth birthday was yesterday, and perhaps because the lines from the Beatles song "When I'm Sixty-Four" kept running through my head, I realized this was an important event for him. We were having friends over for dinner to celebrate, and at breakfast (the one meal when it's OK to have toast), I said quietly but with more culinary conviction than I've ever had, "I'd like to make you a birthday cake."

Michael flinched. "Or we could buy one," he said. "Or ice cream is fine."

"It's time for a cake," I insisted. "We could make it together. I don't think Nancy would mind."

Michael seemed nervous at first, taking out Nancy's old cookbooks and yellowed handwritten recipes, but

I stood my ground. I said, "I think we should bake something new." I took out my computer and googled "easy cakes" and found a Martha Stewart delight that had lots of cocoa and sugar and sour cream.

We began in an uncommon silence we had rarely experienced before in our marriage. For a moment, when Michael held Nancy's sifter, I saw a shadow of sorrow spread across his face, but by the time I was measuring a quarter teaspoon of vanilla into the batter, we were both beaming.

We made the chocolate cake using the right amount of unsweetened chocolate, sour cream, butter, and sugar and with a heavy cream and chocolate glaze. Michael made his grandmother's fried chicken and mashed potatoes and sweet carrots. Our friends brought a delicious salad with walnuts and a subtle ginger vinaigrette.

During dinner Michael and I smiled at each other across the table.

After the candles were lit and we sang "Happy Birthday," Michael sliced the cake, and everybody seemed to enjoy it, even me.

LESSON 9

Revise, Revise,
Revise

I have rewritten, often
several times, every word
I have ever published.
My pencils outlast their erasers.

—*VLADIMIR NABOKOV*

I T CAN TAKE OVER one hundred hours of film to make a two-hour movie. It is the same with the written word. Write and write and write your head off, and then read it aloud to yourself, to friends, and take it out at 2 A.M. and on the train and get it right.

As I was taught in high school, "First it's vision and then it's endless revision." Or as we used to say before computers, "Thread it through the typewriter again."

Now, with computers, it's fine to do much of the editing on the screen, but it's important to print out a whole draft when you think you have it finished, whether it's a poem or an essay or a book. And then you start all over again. Dialogue will be much shorter than you think. Conversations are more like jazz than like what a courtroom stenographer takes down. You will shed some of what you love, and then you will shed some more. Writing is as rigorous as ballet, except you can do it sitting down.

There are two main things I think writers can work on. The first is clarity. So often a student will bring in work, and the opening paragraph meanders around like a shaggy dog. After the piece is read aloud I ask, "What is this about?" Until you know what the story is about and can say it, in one clear sentence, it isn't ready. I must quickly add that it often takes many, many drafts to know what it's about.

The second is transformation. Change is something that is often missing from students' work. I'll see essays, stories, and even whole books that are written well, but have no turning point. The character does not change from the first page to the last. That kind of writing is like riding endlessly along the plains—it's beautiful, but nothing happens. That turning point also often comes after many drafts.

The ten-minute memory assignments I give always

get startling results. Some students continue working on them, and open up the short scenes. Draft after draft, one must roll out the dough and trim it many times to get it right. Moments of brilliance can come with quick writing, but the rigor of rewriting is the challenge.

Basketball

The first time my son met Michael's two boys, they all nodded, said, "Hey," and went off into the summer night to play basketball on a driveway down the street. When they came back sweaty two hours later, I longed to ask the crickets what the boys had talked about. I scanned their tired faces, desperate for a sign. Did they like one another? Would it be OK?

The next morning I asked my son, "What do you think of the big boys?"

"Good," he said.

"Their mother died," I said.

"I know, but they got to know her until they were teenagers. At least they remember their mother."

I had two fears:

1. Of learning to be a family again.
2. Of becoming a widow again.

I admit that in the cold winters of my son's childhood, many nights I let my son sit on the radiator eating macaroni and cheese as we watched *Supernanny*. We were both entranced to see how she solved the problems of all these families, always a husband and wife with unruly children, screaming and carrying on. We were junkies.

Even though the children on the show were holy terrors, they always had two parents. We longed for unruly. In the days after my husband died, my son would march off to preschool and call out, "Get me a new daddy while I'm at school."

Bar

Helen came to class and announced that she had been a journalist for fifty years, that she was not comfortable writing about herself. Indeed, for eight weeks, she never did. Instead she read from a powerful article she was writing on the history of HIV/AIDS. But on the very last day of class, I gave the assignment of "Bar" and asked them to write about it for ten minutes, and she wrote, "My parents both worked long hours, and my sister was bedridden. I, at four years old, went with my older brother to the University of Chicago, every day. I would sit at the back of the class and draw. Afterward, he took me to the local student bar, where I sat up on the stool with the college kids, and I had my milk and cookies. It was my brother who taught me how to read."

After class she presented me with a bouquet of yellow roses. "You remind me of my sister," she said. "She died a long time ago."

I thanked her and asked her sister's name. "Rose," she said, with tears in her eyes. "Her name was Rose."

Stepmother

I am now a stepmother, a title I never dreamed I would have, to two wonderful young men, one with a long red beard, one who once had a streak of blue in his hair. They have told me that they are glad their father married me, and I know how rare that is. Their mother, Nancy, died so suddenly. One day she was teaching art history and sitting on the couch watching a movie with Michael. Then she was sneezing and coughing and feverish, and within twenty-four hours she was dead from sepsis. Nobody knows why. People keep asking why, just as they ask if Willem's cell phone had affected his brain. He didn't have a cell phone. Nancy and Willem are just gone. Sometimes there are no answers.

I now have a new stepmother, whom my father married suddenly at eighty-seven, a few months after his previous wife, Louise, died. Louise was my first stepmother, for thirty years, and I had two stepbrothers and one stepsister, and we had family holidays around a big table. When Willem died Jake and I spent more time there, and my father would let Jake sit on his lap and steer the car on the road back through the woods. Louise died of liver cancer, and my father was wild with grief. He went with a friend to Florida and met a woman, a widow almost his age, and they were wed.

In a sudden and wrenching flurry my father moved from his home to hers, and all traces of my first stepmother vanished. It was like one of those Etch A Sketch screens where everything was shaken and disappeared. It felt like, if not my show, any semblance of a home had been canceled.

Letter

Dear Albert and Owen, Owen and Albert,

Because, to everyone's surprise, I am technically going to be your stepmother, and you are going to be my stepsons, I thought I'd write to you about my thoughts on the subject. I do know we are not the Brady Bunch. We are five people with five distinct ways of viewing the world.

Mainly I hope you find as much joy in your life as you can. Although I never had the honor of meeting your mother, I know she would want that. What role I have in your lives in the future or you in Jake's is anybody's guess.

I do hope we can be there for one another in joyful times, and also in any sorrow to come. Ten years from now, tomorrow, who knows where any of us will be, as we all know.

If you ever want to talk to me, about anything, please do, or just be silent. And I think whatever language "stepmother" is translated in, I believe you're also allowed to tell me when I'm driving you crazy. One of the perks of the job.

All I know is I love your father, I honor your mother, and it's a pleasure getting to know you both.

And as Jake says, "one good thing is we all get more cats."

Bed

Yesterday we put together a double bed from IKEA in the room we now call the boys' room, the same room where we put together a crib from IKEA decades ago, but in fact that was another husband and another time.

Willem and I actually put together the crib. The boys are now "fine young men," as my grandmother would say, who have all gone west to live, in Illinois, Arizona, and California.

We are trying to make the room more "grown-up" for when the boys visit, and we say we are saving so many of their toys, books, and clothes for our grandchildren, but that is not entirely true. It is difficult for us to "put away childish things," not because the boys have asked us to save them, but because these things bear witness to a time nobody else except Nancy and Willem remembers.

The double bed looks good, and it will be just fine for the boys and their girlfriends who sometimes we're told are not girlfriends anymore. The boys have not complained, and I hope the girls (of course I should be saying "women" by now) won't mind all the evidence of childhood.

There is a papier-mâché volcano from preschool on the shelf, made when Willem was still able to walk. And there are those small school uniforms with neckties from South Africa the older boys wore in Johannesburg where Michael was a foreign correspondent and Nancy was an art history professor. Of course we have to keep those buttons that say, "Mandela, the People's Choice."

There is a pair of wooden Dutch shoes along with a tin of dried-up licorice on the desk from our first trip to visit Willem's family in Holland, after we'd taken our journey to Lithuania to adopt our son. And there's that tiny clay replica of the church in Vilnius the cabdriver gave us after that frightening week when the baby had pneumonia and Willem finally found antibiotics that saved his life.

As we put together the double bed, I told Michael how my son used to make meticulous traffic jams with his toy cars from his room to what he called "the mommy-daddy room," and Michael told me how his older son used to say "last day" instead of "yesterday" and how his second son stood up in his crib and said his first word, which was his brother's name.

Trophy

There are trophies on the shelves of the boys' room from every sport under the sun, along with the tiny mortarboard my son wore for the graduation from preschool when I covered my tears with sunglasses. There are the heavy fantasy books that Nancy read patiently to the boys at the dinner table before Michael came home from long hours at the newspaper, and there are the audiotapes Willem made, reading *Curious George* first in Dutch and then in English for when he knew he wouldn't be there. There are the cardboard blocks Willem was able to put together stacked in the corner and all those carved wooden animals from Africa.

Someday the boys might bring home wives and perhaps grandchildren who will play with the toy milk truck from Holland that Willem raced along the wooden floors of the parsonage. Maybe there will be little boys or girls who will wear those school uniforms from South Africa as Halloween costumes.

Last night, before one of our boys arrived with his girlfriend, Michael and I lay on the new bed, staring up at the glow-in-the-dark stars Willem had put up over the crib so many years before. We're definitely going to leave the stars up for when we put a crib in that room again.

As we lay there I recalled the day in 1995 when the Hyakutake Comet passed overhead, and Willem and I saw its bright light even in the city. It wouldn't be back for four hundred years. I remember wondering what it would portend. I was hoping for the arrival of my child. I had no idea of the losses to come as well.

LESSON 10

Be Bold, Be Bolder

Literature is the art of discovering
something extraordinary about ordinary
people, and saying with ordinary words
something extraordinary.

—BORIS PASTERNAK

R EAD IT ONE MORE TIME, and if the opening line
won't knock the reader's socks off, make it so it
does. Do not worry about writing like someone else.
Changing your style is like trying to change your walk.
It is difficult and a waste of time. Your task is to be
more like yourself as a writer. To get really clear, you
have to step to the edge of the cliff and to the edge of
your emotions. In doing so you might almost lose
your mind. Clarity means finding the right words, but
it also means numbering your drafts, so you don't end

up in a heap on the floor with your pages piled in shopping bags, like a wild woman. What you dare not say aloud, put down on paper. Do not concern yourself with whether your words will hurt anyone. They will hurt nobody just by your getting those words from your hand to the page. After you have read your work out loud, sit back down at your writing machine and edit it so you take their breath away.

Being bold happens with revision, and it often comes from anger and often from what you dare not admit you are angry about. It does not matter if you were brought up to be a good girl or to raise hell or whether you would love to jump out of an airplane or are too timid to step out of your house: the only way to reach your reader is to make a wild leap onto the page.

Sometimes when my students get to the most difficult and powerful material, they start by reading it in class and continue on to write whole books. Sometimes, as with a patient leaving a therapist's office with her hand on the doorknob, a student will start to discover what she's been wanting to write on the last day in class.

Umbrella

My father's mother, Dorothy, liked to watch her "games"—the Detroit Tigers on television—all through her nineties. She met my grandfather, Moe, in Canton, Ohio, at a small gathering at a relative's home. Six months later he sent her a card for the Jewish New Year. And then one rainy day he showed up on her porch step.

"When he came to call," she said, "he asked if I would like to go for a stroll, and I accepted, even though it was raining. Then he offered to share his umbrella with me. Now, I *had* my own umbrella," said Dorothy, "but with Moe I knew that was a proposal."

I heard most of my father's stories about his mother as he got older. I was sitting in a hospital waiting room with him, waiting to hear the surgeon's verdict on his second wife's health. What could a fifty-five-year-old widow say to her eighty-three-year-old father that he didn't already know? The fact was, not much. It was he who began to open up about his life, how he wore long trousers to cover his heavy brace in an era when all the other boys wore shorts and they would pick up his pant leg and point. I realized that, because I asked my students to write about food, I knew more about curry-scented breezes in New Delhi or standing in a garden in Nebraska with a salt shaker eating ripe tomatoes off the vine or sneaking out at 3 A.M. with a sandwich in the Dodge because a father forbade a girl to take the wheel than I did about my own father's life.

Pictures

"Everything is going up" is what my great-grandfather Max, a button salesman from Poland, used to say when he rode his horse and cart selling his wares in Ohio. When my father's father would leave his hat on the bed, that was the sign for my great-grandmother to make love that night. I have a brown-and-white photograph of my great-grandfather holding my great-grandmother's hand. They look steadily into the camera, and he is wearing his hat.

Even when my son was sobbing in the closet, holding onto a sleeve of one of his father's coats after he died, I had the strong sense that we were alive, that we had some time left to live. Those dark days my humor was fierce, and I had to control myself to keep from asking one of the salesclerks at IKEA whether they sold simple but elegant pinewood coffins, because they said they had everything for every stage of life.

I constantly have images in my head. Sometimes they are pictures or sensations: the back page of *Life* magazine my brother kept in his room because it had a photo of an ice-hockey goalie's face covered in all the stitches he would have had if he hadn't worn a mask; the feel of the tight panty girdle I wore at ballroom dancing class as a ten-year-old; the warm washcloth on my face when my Michigan grandmother visited and gave me a bath. Sometimes they are audio memories: I hear my son saying, "I guess God ran out of numbers" the night his father died or my father telling me, "Hitch yourself to a star, and you remain a wagon."

I will be sitting at my desk, and I will be transported back to an ice-covered pond with red autumn maple leaves frozen beneath the surface, with my mother teaching my brother, my sister, me, and my father how to skate.

I awake in the middle of the night, not knowing what to do with my parents' wedding album, its padded cover faded white, which sits, confused, on my shelf, even though they got divorced forty-two years ago.

Pajamas

My father talked about writing jokes for live radio in a room at the Rockefeller Center and the day he cut flowers from his neighbor's garden when he was seven years old and tried to sell them back to his neighbor. He couldn't stop talking and told me about wearing pajamas under his clothes to school to make the kids laugh instead of tease when they lifted his pant leg. He talked to me of taking long walks on Saturdays when he was a child to watch sandlot baseball games because as observant Jews they could not ride in a car on the Sabbath. And that day he repeated what I had said at my first husband's funeral, "It is not a calamity to die with dreams unfulfilled, but it is a calamity not to dream," a quote from the educator Benjamin E. Mays. And now that his memory is being erased, it is I who am the keeper of his past.

Illness

And now researchers are saying that the polio virus that attacked my father and withered his leg when he was a little boy can be put into the brain cancer, the glioblastoma that killed Willem, and can possibly save people's lives.

Apron

When I assigned the topic of "Apron," one woman who had missed half the classes wrote: "My mother wore a red and white checked full apron every day of her life, and when she died I stayed up ironing her aprons, as if that would make her come back to life. She always looked like a dowdy housewife, at least to me. She embarrassed me. When I cleaned out her house, I found all this lacy underwear, not just sexy underwear, but slightly pornographic, with cutouts at the nipples and crotch. My father had left when I was eight. I don't know when she wore them. I wish I could have asked her."

From then on she never missed a class.

Paper

My grandfather, my mother's father, started a paper company he named Baldwin, "because Baldwin is a good, clean word" was what he always said. He had found it in the phone book after he went through names beginning with A. But only this week, I discovered a letter he'd written to my mother in a box of old papers I'd saved in the back of my closet.

I stood in the closet and read, "I also chose the word Baldwin because it had WIN in the name. WORDS MATTER KIDDO," he wrote.

First Job

A woman with twisted hands and an English accent, who appeared to be in her eighties, sat in class and matter-of-factly read aloud what she had written: "I was in London during the War, and I worked with the carrier pigeons. I typed the secret messages that were taped to the birds' legs. Every time those birds flew out into the world I had the feeling I was with them."

I nodded my head and thanked her. I understood.

Telephone

My mother, who is ninety, is the last person I know who calls me on my landline, which both of us call "the regular phone." I talk to her at least once a day, sometimes twice, on her regular phone. Although my mother lives in an apartment in one city and I live in an apartment in another, we often talk about my childhood house where we had a yellow phone affixed firmly to the flowered-wallpaper wall in the kitchen and a heavy black phone on the night table in my parents' bedroom.

There was a telephone etiquette that we strictly adhered to, although it was never spoken out loud. Never call before 9 A.M. On Sundays, never call before 10. Never call during dinner hours. And never, ever call after 10 P.M. Unless there is an emergency.

My mother tutors students in reading, avidly follows politics, takes three-mile walks, cleans her own house, and drives.

"This is she," she would say in our old house, using a slightly higher voice than usual, when she answered the wall phone in the kitchen. I was supposed to say, "May I ask who's calling, please?" when I answered and it was for someone else in the family.

I joke with my mother about how strange it would have been if everyone carried their heavy black dial phones with them whenever they left home, the way we do with our cellular devices, or used them to take pictures.

Pumpkin

This morning my mother and I talked on the regular phone about walking into the quiet house before we had an answering machine, before anything blinked or beeped. My mother would stand at the kitchen table humming as she sorted through the mail.

We like to play a game called "Remembering the House." Remember when we hollowed out the big pumpkin for my brother to wear on his head on Halloween, but it was so heavy he had to push it around in a wheelbarrow? Remember when the door of the blue Buick station wagon fell off in the driveway? Remember when we could hear the deer clambering up the snowy back steps in February? I remember answering the kitchen phone and learning our friend's mother had just killed herself.

Landlines are supposedly good in disasters. You might lose connection to the cell tower, but you can have a connection to the outside world, if that world still exists. The truth is, I do cling to my regular phone as a lifeline, not in case of a national or international emergency in the future, but for a connection to the past.

My mother says, "Remember when that boy Andy would call and you'd answer the kitchen phone and twirl, wrapping the cord around you, and then untwirl the cord like you kids were at a dance?"

One summer night I was with a boy in the woods. My mother shouted in a singsong voice from the back porch, "Sweetheart, it's for you!" and I scrambled to button my blouse.

My brother, sister, and I often heard the nuns laughing as they played basketball on the macadam court in the convent next door while we raked autumn leaves. We'd faintly hear the phone ring and then race inside to see who could answer it first. I remember how, after the divorce, my mother would talk quietly to men on the phone in her bedroom as I pressed my ear hard to the closed door.

After the last phone call ever with my mother, will I keep the regular phone? Even if I disconnect it, I believe I shall keep it on the shelf, along with my beloved Smith Corona typewriter. I know there will be times when I will hear a phantom ring, even after the cord is severed. I will pick up the receiver as if it were a conch shell found on the beach, and I will say, "This is she. Remember?"

Afterword

We write to taste life twice,
in the moment and in retrospect.

—*ANAÏS NIN*

MY PARENTS HAVE NEVER talked about their wedding day to us kids. I will never know that story. Now neither remembers why they got divorced, but I stubbornly cling to the wedding album like a child holding onto a garish stuffed animal won at an amusement park.

Last week, on the day of what would have been my parents' sixty-fifth wedding anniversary, my mother called my father, and they spoke lovingly to each other for forty-five minutes. They both called me afterward. They both said, "We laughed and laughed. It was a wonderful talk. We talked about skating in the backyard."

In my mother's final years she has a new way of looking at the world. Everything she sees or hears or reads she thinks she has seen or heard or read before, a sort of déjà vu magnified, as if the tape in the recorder has been used up and plays the same scenes over and over again. Perhaps there is nothing new under the sun, and yet as writers we have to "make it new," as Ezra Pound said, "make it new."

I had a student who was in the same concentration camp as his psychiatrist. When I asked what got them through, he said, "All we had are our stories. I spent most of my life before the camps being worried about the future. Now I have no time for that. Now instead I say, 'I look forward to each day with curiosity.'"

I used to have students who would discreetly pull the cuffs over their concentration camp numbers on their wrists. Now I have students on whose necks I can see inked butterflies when they bend their heads to write in class, but every day when I enter the classroom I hear my son's words: "Give me something to dream about. Give me something to dream about."

Acknowledgments

Great thanks to my early readers and writers, Denver Butson, Michael Hill, and Carol Weston; to my agent, Malaga Baldi, who has stood by for so long; to my editor, Jennifer Urban-Brown—working with her continues to be a wonderful dance; and to assistant editor Julia Gaviria, who has gracefully pushed me to run the pages through the typewriter one more time.

List of Assignments

This list includes the prompts in the text and more. Take out a pen and paper, or your computer, or even your phone, if you write on that. Set a timer for ten minutes and select a word from the list. Write wherever your hand takes you when you think of this word, but do not get up from the chair until the timer rings. Do not fret if you write only a few lines. Do not fret if you don't think it's good or interesting or what you thought you would write. Do not fret. You have begun to write your story. When my son used to see me doing this at the kitchen table, he would say, "Stop that scribble-scrabble," but after you have done two hundred scribble-scrabbles, your story will begin to take shape, and when that happens, you can begin to shape your story.

Apron

Bar

Basketball

Bed

Bicycle

Birthday

Boat

Broom

Button

Cake

Car

Chair

Chlorine

Church, Temple,
  or Mosque

Concert

Cookbook

Couch

Dancing

Desk

Dessert

Dining Room
  Table

Diploma

Divorce

Door

Dream

Emergency Room

Envelope

Eyebrows

First Apartment

First Job

Food

Game

Garden

Gloves

Great-Grand-
  parent

Guidebook

Gun

Gym Class

Hair

Hands

Hat

High Heels

Honeymoon

Hood

Hospital

Hotel

Humming

Ice-Skating

Illness

Kitchen Table

Knife

Laundry

Letter

Library

Lunch

Mail

Moon

Movie

Moving

Museum

Music

Music Lesson

Name

Necklace

Neighbor

Nightgown

Notebook

October

Office

Pajamas

Paper

Party

Pencil

Perfume

Phone Book

Photograph

Pictures

Pipe

Playground

Prayers

Recipes

Ribbon

Rice

Road

Saltwater

Sandwich

School

Sewing
Sister
Shoes
Slippers
Snow
Snowstorm
Soccer
Soup
Stairs
Stamp

Stepmother
Straws
Studio
Stuffed Animal
Summer Job
Tattoos
Telephone
Tennis Court
Test
Theater

Train
Trophy
Typewriter
Umbrella
Vietnam
War
Washing Machine
Widow
Window

MICHAEL HILL

About the Author

PATTY DANN is the author of three novels, *Starfish,
Mermaids,* and *Sweet & Crazy.* She has also published two
memoirs, *The Goldfish Went on Vacation: A Memoir of Loss
(and Learning to Tell the Truth about It)* and *The Baby Boat:
A Memoir of Adoption.* Her work has been translated into
French, German, Italian, Portuguese, Dutch, Chinese,
Korean, and Japanese. *Mermaids* was made into a movie
starring Cher, Winona Ryder, and Christina Ricci.

Her articles have appeared in the *New York Times;*
the *Chicago Tribune;* the *Boston Globe;* the *Philadelphia
Inquirer;* the *Christian Science Monitor; O, the Oprah Maga-
zine;* the *Oregon Quarterly; Redbook; More; ForbesWoman;
Poets & Writers Magazine; The Writer's Handbook; Dirt:
The Quirks, Habits, and Passions of Keeping House;* and
This I Believe: On Motherhood.

Dann has an MFA in writing from Columbia University
and a BA from the University of Oregon. She has taught at
Sarah Lawrence College and the West Side YMCA in New
York City.